CAROLINE COUNTY MARYLAND

Marriages, Births and Deaths

1850–1880

F. Edward Wright

HERITAGE BOOKS
2015

HERITAGE BOOKS

AN IMPRINT OF HERITAGE BOOKS, INC.

Books, CDs, and more—Worldwide

For our listing of thousands of titles see our website
at
www.HeritageBooks.com

Published 2015 by
HERITAGE BOOKS, INC.
Publishing Division
5810 Ruatan Street
Berwyn Heights, Md. 20740

International Standard Book Numbers
Paperbound: 978-1-58549-773-7
Clothbound: 978-0-7884-6105-7

CAROLINE COUNTY

MARRIAGES, BIRTHS, AND DEATHS

1850 - 1880

This information was extracted from newspapers, the Federal Mortality Schedules, and the County Court Records of births and deaths.

Abstracts have been made from copies of Caroline County newspapers on file at the Enoch Pratt Free Library, Baltimore. Aside from a few duplicative copies at the Maryland Historical Society there are no other known copies extant. A few items for earlier periods, prior to 1850, have been taken from Easton newspapers. The Caroline newspapers in circulation prior to 1880 are listed below followed by the code used for reference in this publication. Dates given are the dates the newspaper was founded.

Caroline Intelligencer (CI)................1831
Caroline Advocate.................prior to 1835
Denton Pearl (DP)...............September 1840
Denton Journal (DJ)..............prior to 1850
American Union (AU)..................July 1860
Federalsburg Courier.............February 1872

Part Two of this book lists the mortality schedules recorded in the federal censuses of 1850, 1860, 1870 and 1880. To determine how fully deaths were reported, a comparison was made of the deaths reported by the papers from 1 June 1869 to 1 June 1870, the same period covered by the 1870 mortality schedule. Fortunately all issues of the American Union, overlapped by issues of the Denton Journal, were available. There were 101 deaths listed in the mortality schedule and 54 deaths reported in the weekly papers; of these deaths, 26 were noted in both sources. This indicates that there about 200 actual deaths occurring in Caroline County during this twelve-month period.

Part Three lists the court records of birth and death, 1865 - 1885, which were required to be reported by state law, although largely ignored. Of the approximately 200 deaths estimated in the above paragraph only one was reported in the County Courthouse Records, now held by the Hall of Records, Annapolis. An article in the American Union (14 January 1869) illustrates this same lack of adherence to the state law, referring to the 1868 records,

"The records in the Clerks office show 104 marriage licenses issued during the (past year)... 19 births and 10 deaths (were) recorded. Of all the births and deaths not nearly one-half were recorded, many persons being ignorant that the laws of this state require the recording of each birth and death within six months after the occurrence (under) penalty of $5.00."

Comments or questions are welcomed.

F. Edward Wright

Abbreviations used

Balt - Baltimore	mo - month
co - county	Phila - Philadelphia
d - died	QA - Queen Anne's
das - days	res - residence or resided
Dorch - Dorchester	s/o - son of
d/o - daughter of	Talb - Talbot
m - married	yrs - years

PART ONE

Newspaper Abstracts of Deaths and Marriages

CI 30 Aug 1831/Death of Henry Stubbs Collison, "a young man of our acquaintance
- He was in the very prime of life..."

DP 30 Sep 1840/In Denton on 19 Sep Elizabeth Catherine Mezick d, d/o Mr. James
R. and Elenor Mezick age 2 yrs, 1 mo and 17 das

DP 28 Mar 1846/D in Caroline Co 18 Mar Thomas Coke, youngest s/o John and Mary
E. Beachamp age 2 yrs, 10 mos and 1 day

AU 17 Jul 1860/Drowned Fri evening 13 Jul last about 5 o'clock at Chestertown
in Chester River, Robert eldest s/o Capt Robert Emerson of Caroline Co while
bathing. He was the only s/o the Captain by his first wife; age about 16 yrs.

AU 24 Jul 1860/On Wed last 18 Jul Alexander Saulsbury in superintending the
operation of his wheat thresher on the farm of James Rickards a few miles from
town (Denton) met with a most painful accident by which he may lose one of his
hands. Dr. Harmon of Denton dressed the hand.

M at res of Capt Levi Dukes 17 Jul by Rev William M. Warner, William A. Barton
Esq of Caroline Co and Mrs. Carrie Barton at Talb Co.

D in Hillsborough Fri, 20 Jul, Henry Catrip age about 22 yrs

AU 14 Aug 1860/M 9 Aug at M.E. Church Concord by Rev T. Numbers, William R.
Peters to Mrs. S. E. Todd both of Caroline Co.

D in Greensobourh 21 Jul, Ethland infant child of Edgar and Elizabeth A.
Plummer, age 11 mos and 4 das.

AU 21 Aug 1860/The wife of Mr. Charles M. Jump living in the Chapel District
came near losing her life on Tues last 14 Aug by the gore of a cow.

D in Centreville 4 Aug, Mary Eldora infant d/o Edward T. and Mary N. Willis,
age 6 mos and 17 das.

D 16 Aug Mary Anna d/o John W. and Hester Christopher age 11 mos and 5 das.

AU 28 Aug 1860/D near Hillsborough Sun 26 Aug, John Wesley youngest s/o John
W. and Emily Knotts, age 8 months.

AU 4 Sep 1860/D at his res in first election district of the county, George
Ross age about 28.

D near New Hope in the fourth district 26 Aug Jane Willis youngest d/o Joseph
Willis deceased, age 32.

D 17 Aug Charles Dean s/o Charles and Mary Dean, 8 yrs, 7 mos, 7 das.

D at the res of Esrah Hitch in Tuakahoe Neck 1 Sep, Miss Catherine Gray, age
about 20.

AU 11 Sep 1860/Aaron Wilson d in Denton 4 Sep suddenly of apoplexy; he was one
of our "mostly highly esteemed and venerable citizens," age about 66 yrs.

Fri 31 Aug Mrs. Sherman, wife of Capt Thomas B. Sherman d near East New
Market, in Dorch Co.

AU 18 Sep 1860/M at the bride's res 11 Sep by Rev W. M. Warner, Warner R.
Busteed Esq of this county and Mrs. Anna E. Hoxter of Easton, Talb Co.

AU 25 Sep 1860/M in city of Wilmington 10 Sep by Rev Charles S. Breck, Joshua
Seward to Miss Mary W. Williams, both of Caroline Co.

Newspaper Abstracts

M 10 Sep by Rev W. E. England, Daniel Orrell and Miss Annie M. Coursey, both of this county.

AU 9 Oct 1860/M Mon 13 Oct at the ME Episcopal Church Centreville by Rev James E. Bryan, Capt Henry J. Strandberg of Easton and Mrs. Caroline A. Seegar of Centreville.

Mr. Edward Carmean d at his home in Caroline Co 2 Oct.

Mrs. Ann Hopper wid of the late Judge P. B. Hopper d in Centreville Tues morning 2 Oct, leaving a large circle of relatives and friends to mourn her loss.

Mahala youngest d/o Isaac Mason d Tues evening 2 Oct at the res of her father near Ruthsburg, age 15 yrs.

AU 23 Oct 1860/M 18 Oct at the res of William Lockerman by Rev William M. Warner, Mr. Abraham Y. Collins and Miss Sallie A. Long both of this county.

M 16 Oct by Rev Thomas Numbers, William H. Willey of Sussex Co Del and Miss Bell J. Melony of Caroline Co.

M Thurs 18 Oct by Rev T. Numbers, Capt N. J. Corkran and Miss Irena Blades both of this county.

Charles Cottingham d at his res near Denton Tues 16 Oct after a protracted illness, age 53. "...an estimable citizen and possessed many virtues..."

AU 30 Oct 1860/Noah Murphy, aged about 48 yrs, of Federalsburg d very suddenly Sat morning 20 Oct in consequence of a severe wound on the head and face sustained the afternoon previous, on board the schooner Two Brothers on the Nanticoke ..(missing) ... caught him up and dashed him with such violence against the wooden deck as to render him entriely speechless. A physician was soon obtained but the wounds proved fatal. He was brought up by water to Crotcher's Ferry and buried near there on Sun afternoon following. He leaves a wife and four children, one of whom is deaf and dumb.

M Thurs 18 Oct by Rev E. Miller, Joshua W. Bryant of Denton to Miss Sallie, eldest d/o the late Clinton Cook of Centreville.

Solomon Melvin d at his res near Burrsville in Caroline Co 19 Oct.

Robert Morgan d at res of Jacob Morgan in Talb Co 27 Oct, age about 26 yrs.

Mrs. Lydia Satterfield d suddenly at her res at the Beaver Dam in QA Co Fri night last, age 73 yrs.

AU 6 Nov 1860/M 19 Aug by Rev T. P. Williams, Joseph W. Records of Sussex Co, Del, to Miss Margaret Sorden of Caroline Co.

AU 13 Nov 1860/M Wed 24 Oct at the ME parsonage, Princess Anne, by Rev A. Wallice, Reese Morgan editor of the Saulsbury Sentinel to Miss Louisa A. Collier of Saulsbury, Somerset Co.

M 8 Nov by Rev Thomas Numbers, William Sorden and Miss Sara Rickards, both of Caroline Co.

M 1 Nov By Rev Thomas Numbers, William Wheeler and Miss Susan Davis both of Caroline Co.

Short A. Willis d at his res in the third dist 6 Nov, age 18.

AU 13 Dec 1860/Capt Thomas Davis was drowned Mon night week while on his way from Denton Bridge to his home, two miles above Denton. He is supposed to have fallen from a small canoe in which he left the bridge about 6 o'clock in the evening.

M 30 Oct by Rev Jesse Shreeve, D. S. Moore and Miss Annie E. Connolly, both of Caroline Co.

M 6 Dec by Rev McCarty, Thomas Eaton and Miss Willie Patchett, both of Caroline Co.

M 22 Nov by Rev E. England, Rev T. S. Williams of the Phila Conference ME Church and Miss Emily Bell d/o Thomas Bell of Caroline Co.

Mrs. Hubbard wife of William Hubbard d Mon last 10 Dec in Caroline Co.

AU 20 Dec 1860/M this morning by Rev McClarey, John W. Todd to Miss Lydia T. Patton, all of this county.

Bennett Franklin s/o James M. and Catharine Whitby near Greensborough, aged 5 yrs and 2 mos d 4 Dec of diptheria.

AU 27 Jun 1861/John L. McCombs formerly of Denton d at St. Louis Mo 15 Jun of consumption.

AU 1 Sep 1864/Thomas F. Corkran res near Gilpins Point in this county, last week manumitted all his negroes.

DJ 28 Apr 1866/James S. Breeding d 10 Apr age 67.

AU 17 Jan 1867/M in Hillsborough 10 Jan...(missing)..S. T. Gardner, Corporal George C. Sher...U. S. Army and Miss Mary A. Bush d/o John C. Bush.

AU 31 Jan 1867/M 31 Dec by Rev John Hough, Daniel Gibbins and Miss Anna Jane Harris, all of this county.

M 10 Jan by Rev John Hough, Samuel M. Jewell and Francis J. Hobbs, all of this county.

M 23 Jan by Rev John Hough, Samuel R. Boulden and Annie Wallace.

M 24 Jan by Rev John Irwin, John F. Eaton and Mrs. Mary E. Tuff, both of this co.

M 24 Jan by Rev R. W. Todd, Samuel C. Scott of Talb Co and Miss E. Jester of Caroline Co.

AU 7 Feb 1867/M 25 Dec in Union Grove M.P. Church by Rev B. F. Benson, Leonard Willis and Miss Sarah E. Covey, all of this county.

M 23 Jan by Rev B. F. Benson, F. Theadore Perry of Newcastle Co, Del and Miss Martha L. Thomas d/o of the late John B. Thomas of QA Co.

M at the res of L. H. C. Davis 29 Jan by Rev B. F. Benson, Robert A. Connaway and Miss Elizabeth W. Dail, all of this county.

M 29 Jan by Rev S. Gardner, James Jarrell and Miss Mollie C. Busteed, all of this county.

AU 21 Feb 1867/M 24 Jan at the res of the bride's father by Rev S. Powers, James T. Hynson and Miss Martha J. Clendenning, both of this county.

M at the res of the bride's father in Newton Md 12 Feb by Rev Jesse Shreeve, J. D. A. Robinson of this county and Mrs. Sarah Sudler.

Mrs. Ann Rochester d in Denton Sat night 16 Feb, age 70 yrs.

Newspaper Abstracts

AU 28 Feb 1867/M 5 Jan by Rev P. H. Rawlings, Twiford N. Wright of this
county and Lina W., d/o Daniel B. Kinder of Sussex Co, Del.

M 19 Jan by Rev P. H. Rawlings, John Rhoads of this county and Anna Milman
of Sussex Co, Del.

M 7 Feb by Rev P. H. Rawlings, Wellington Patton and Ellen Francis Hancock all
of Sussex Co, Del.

M at the res of the bride's mother 14 Feb by Rev S. T. Gardner, William Massey
and Miss Sarah Cahall, both of this county.

AU 7 Mar 1867/M 28 Feb at the res of the bride's parents by Rev John Hough,
Jacob Alburger and Miss Sara Terry, all of this county.

AU 21 Mar 1867/"On Friday night last, 15 March, one of the most horrible
murders that ever was committed in this county...perpetrated upon Mr. James
A. Tarr... respected citizen of Hillsborough..." He was killed in bed (throat
cut) and robbed of $200 to $300.

AU 28 Mar 1867/John H. Dukes age about 48 d at his res in the first dist Fri
last, 22 Mar.

Miss Mary Breeding age 21 d at the home of her mother in Caroline Co on 2 Mar.

AU 11 Apr 1867/The death of Josiah Jump is announced, a res of Denton and
Clerk of the Circuit Court for Caroline Co. For several months he has been
confined to his bed. He was interred at the family burial place near
Jumptown on Wed morning. He was 47 yrs old.

Mrs. Esther Selby d/o of the late John Bell d in Balt 6 Apr, age about 35.

AU 18 Apr 1867/Maria Dawson near Greensboro d Mon 11 Mar, age 74.

Charles W., infant s/o A. A. and Candace R. Griffith d 6 Apr age 2 yrs, 11
mos, 13 das.

AU 2 May 1867/Jacob Trice age about 22 yrs d suddenly of pneumonia 22 Apr.

AU 9 May 1867/William Ross age about 45 d at his res in Greensborough 2 May.

Matilda H. Chambers wife of Henry P. Chambers and d/o Thomas Haven of Phila
d at Federalsburg 2 May, age 33.

AU 16 May 1867/M 8 May at the bride's father's home by Rev Joseph L. Kenney,
James W. Davis and Miss Annie C. Davis, eldest d/o Rev Ed. Davis, all of this
county.

AU 30 May 1867/M at the res of the bride's mother on the evening of 23 May by
Rev William B. Tolan, J. Marion Emerson editor of the American Union and Miss
Lizzie N. Stewart of Gloucester County, New Jersey.

William Hall, age about 57, d suddenly 21 May at his res in Halltown.

AU 6 Jun 1867/H. P. Gootee of Balt and Dr. Benjamin Gootee of Smyrna Del are
on a visit to Preston called by the extreme illness of their brother, William
H. Gootee who it's thought is past all hope of recovery.

M 29 May by Rev John Hough, John Beachamp and Miss Elizabeth Horsey, all of
this county.

M 29 May by Rev John Hough, Andrew L. Hutchinson and Miss Willemina McNash,
both of this county.

AU 13 Jun 1867/M 30 May at the res of the bride's parents by Rev William

-4-

Newspaper Abstracts

O'Neill, W. P. Roe and Miss Martha J. Graham, all of this county.

Mrs. Martha Voss, age 75, 10 mos, 2 das, d at the home of her son James Voss in Kent Co, Del, 2 Jun. "She was a faithful and consistent member of the M.E. Church from the days of her youth."

AU 20 Jun 1867/M 11 Jun by Rev G. F. Beavon, C. F. Cockran of Middletown Del and Miss Corine B., d/o Robert E. Hardcastle of this county.

Luella Medora youngest child of Edward and S. Willa. Pritchett age 2 yrs and 6 mos d in Denton Mon evening last, 17 Jun.

Noah Seward age 67 d at his res in the 1st dist 26 May.

AU 27 Jun 1867/William B. Colgan was divorced from Margaret R. Colgan, formerly Margaret R. Davis 19 Jun.

John Golt was divorced from Mary E. Golt formerly Mary E. Seward.

M at the bride's res 17 Jun by Rev McCauley, John M. Collison of Sussex Co Del and Mrs. Margaret A. Dukes of Georgetown D. C.

William H. Gootee a well and respected citizen of this county d in Preston on 13 Jun, age 49.

AU 4 Jul 1867/M last Thurs evening 27 Jun in Denton by Rev R. W. Todd, Thomas A. Smith and Mrs. Sara R. Byrne.

AU 11 Jul 1867/M 4 Jul by Rev Robert W. Todd, Jessee Lewis and Mrs. Mary Wilson, both of this county.

M 29 Jun by Rev Robert W. Todd, Richard M. Busteed and Mrs. Eliza J. Williams all of this county.

M 1 Jul in Greensborough by Rev William O'Neill, Rufus Monchmon of Wilmington Del and Miss Carry B. Genn of Greensboro.

James Gooding age about 50 d in Hillsborough 4 Jul of consumption.

D in Denton 17 Jun Herbert Southerland age 3 yrs and 3 mos and on 2 Jul Maggie age 9 mos and 13 das, son and daugher of Rev B. F. Benson.

AU 18 Jul 1867/"Moses Coker an old colored citizen of this county died at his residence in the first district last week aged 103 years. He was respected by our white citizens who knew him as a man of truth, promptness and punctuality in all his dealings. He had acquired considerable property, owning at the time of his death some 3 or 4 famrs - His estate is estimated at about $15000 which he leaves to his children and grandchildren."

Mrs. Mary Fisher wife of George Fisher, age 63, d in Dorch Co where she had gone on a visit on 12 Jul.

AU 25 Jul 1867/M at the P.E. Church in Hillsborough 16 Jul by Rev B. F. Beavon, William T. Elliott and Miss Nettie Zook, all of this county.

AU 8 Aug 1867/William G. Nicholson a res of Denton was stricken with paralysis in his left hand on Sat last, 3 Aug. He holds a position at the Customs of Balt.

George M. Whitby, age about 27, d in the first dist 27 Jul.

AU 12 Sep 1867/"Mr. Addison Hardcastle, a merchant of St Louis, d suddenly in New York City on Thursday night last 5 August. The deceased was a native of this town - a son of the late Edward B. Hardcastle, who 27 years ago was the

Newspaper Abstracts

principal merchant of this place and who died suddenly in 1842. Addison Hardcastle was a brother of Capt. Edward L. F. Hardcastle now a citizen of Talbot County."

Mrs. Sara Ann wife of Job D. A. Robins age about 23 d 24 Aug at Potters Landing.

Mrs. Annie E. wife of John W. Knotts and d/o Jesse Hubbard age 32 d near Hillsborough 20 Aug.

AU 19 Sep 1867/"John Williams a son of Mr. Baynard Williams aged about 20 years residing near Upper Hunting Creek in this county was drowned at Upper Hunting Creek Mill on Saturday last 14 September. It is believed he was laboring under abberations of mind, left his father's house, went to the mill pond and by some means unaccounted for got into the water and drowned..."

M 10 Sep by Rev J. Hough, Robert Burns and Miss Annie Griffin, all of this county.

M 10 Sep by Rev J. Hough, William E. Frampton and Miss Mary E. Nichols, both of this county.

M at the res of the bride's mother in Denton Tues night last 17 Sep by Rev B. F. Benson, R. H. Cunningham and Miss Annie E. Collins.

AU 26 Sep 1867/On 16 Sep a divorce was granted in the case of Susan E. See versus James See.

AU 3 Oct 1867/Joseph Baker age 48 d in Denton Fri last 27 Sep of lockjaw. M Tues last 1 Oct at Vernon Del by Rev J. Hough, Tilghman Nuttle of this county and Mrs. Emeline Taylor of Kent Co Del.

M Thurs last 26 Sep by Rev Thomas Numbers, Levin W. Pool and Miss Mollie J. Pierce, all of this county.

AU 17 Oct 1867/Jacob Charles age 87 yres and 3 mos d at his res in Federalsburg on Tues night 15 Oct last after a short illness. (His obituary appears in the following issue of 24 Oct.): He was born in Dorch Co in 1780 and res there during early manhood. Fifty-two yrs ago he removed to Federalsburg and engaged in merchandising and continued for 40 yrs there closing a life of integrity and honor without manifest disease in the calm and assured peacefulness of the Christian. Reared in the Society of Friends it was not until about 30 yrs since that he connected himself with the M.E. Church. A widow, six children and more than a score of grandchildren sorrow..."
AU 31 Oct 1867/Sarah E. Peters wife of William R. Peters d in Kent Co Del 12 Oct age 26.

AU 7 Nov 1867/M 1 Nov Dr. J. V. Knotts and Miss Kate O. Cooper both of Templeville.

Mrs. Mary Nexia Stafford age 80 yrs and 4 mos d Tues 22 Oct at the res of son William H. Stafford.

AU 14 Nov 1867/Alex Greenley age about 37 d at Hillsborough Thurs last 7 Nov.

AU 21 Nov 1867/M at the M.E. parsonage Greensborough 29 Oct by Rev William O'Neill, James P. Longfellow of this county and Mrs. Catharine Cooper of Kent Co Del

AU 28 Nov 1867/M 14 Nov at the res of the bride's mother by Rev William O'Neill John F. Straughn to Miss Mary Jane Norriss, all of this county.

Newspaper Abstracts

William Delahay only child of the Hon. John F. Dawson of Caroline Co d 7 Nov age 3 yrs and 6 mos.

Nemiah Clark of Delaware Lodge Number 1, IOOF of Wilmington Del d in Greensborough 14 Nov after a lingering illness of consumption and buried here. The funeral was attended with the honors of Kenchel Lodge Number 27 IOOF of Greensborough Md.

AU 5 Dec 1867/M 14 Nov by Rev J. Hough, T. W. Ringold and Miss Martha Hubbard, all of this county.

M 27 Nov by Rev J. Hough, James E. Douglass and Mrs. Emma Clark, all of this county.

M at the res of the bride's mother on 28 Nov by Rev William O'Neill, James D. Wilson and Miss Mary Swan, all of this county.

Mrs. Sallie M. Stafford consort of William H. Stafford of this county d Wed 27 Nov after a short but painful illness, age 28 yrs and 7 mos. "She in her early years connected herself with the M. E. Church."

Shadrack J. Raughley of Tuckahoe Neck has been admitted to the bar as a practicing attorney in Del. He was a student under the Hon. Willard Saulsbury.

AU 12 Dec 1867/M 27 Nov by Rev George F. Beavon, W. Frank Gadd and Miss Julia A. Morgan, Both of this county.

M 27 Nov by Rev R. W. Todd, John R. Morgan and Miss Martha Simpson, all of this county.

M at the res of the bride's father on 5 Dec by Rev B. F. Benson, Truston M. Wright and Miss Julia E. Stafford, all of this county.

Mrs. Elizabeth Ferrins d at her res near Burrsville 9 Dec age about 50.

DJ 18 Jan 1868/M 31 Dec at the M.E. parsonage Greensborough by Rev William O'Neill, James S. Edwards to Miss Eliza Cooper, all of Kent Co Del.

M by Rev William O'Neill 31 Dec at the res of the bride's brother, Thomas Potts to Miss Mary B. Orrell, all of this county.

M by Rev William O'Neill at the M. E. parsonage Greensborough 8 Jan, P. C. Thomas to Miss Emeline Porter of Caroline Co.

Miss Laura Harris age 31 d at the res of her mother near Preston 2 Jan.

Jacob L. Zook age 48 d at his res near Denton 11 Jan.

DJ 25 Jan 1868/Mrs. Elizabeth Gill age 77 was found dead in bed Wed morning last 22 Jan. She was a consistent member of the M.E. Church.

M in St. Pauls Chapel Hillsborough 27 Nov by Rev George F. Beaven, William F. Gadd and Julia A. d/o Jacob Morgan, both of this county.

DJ 29 Aug 1868/M at the res of the bride's father 18 Dec by Rev George F. Beaven, Eugene M. Bonwill of QA Co and Linda Pennington of Caroline Co.

M in Hillsboro 1 Jan by Rev George F. Beaven, William J. Wilkinson and Mollie E. Anderson, both of Caroline Co.

M at the res of the bride's mother 9 Jan by Rev George F. Beaven, William Barcus of QA Co and Sara Ann Carter of Caroline Co.

M at the res of Captain Peter Collins 9 Jan by Rev B. F. Benson, Nicholas S. Hopkins to Emma Wright.

M at the res of the bride's father by Rev R. W. Todd 21 Jan, William R. Butler to Miss Kate Wood, both of this county.

DJ 1 Feb 1868/M 30 Jan by Rev B. F. Benson, Zebdiah Fountain to Miss Sue H. Knotts, both of this county.

M by Rev B. F. Benson, Beachamp Layton to Miss Georgellender Reed.

Ignatus Lednum age 80 d at his res in Denton 25 Jan.

Mrs. Margaret Cahall age 56 d 18 Jan at Galena.

DJ 8 Feb 1868/M 14 Jan at the M. E. parsonage in Greensborough by Rev William O'Neill, James H. Mitchell to Miss Maggie More, all of this county.

M 30 Jan at the res of the bride's mother by Rev R. W. Todd, James E. Wright and Miss Mollie E. Cooper, all of this county.

M at Locust Grove at the res of the bride's father 5 Feb by Rev George F. Beaven, Thomas Corkran of New Castle Co Del and Margaret M. d/o Robert E. Hardcastle of Caroline Co.

Margaret E. Wyatt wife of Thomas H. Wyatt age 29 yrs and 21 das d 22 Jan after a lingering affliction.

Robert Emmett s/o James M. and Catharine Whitby age 6 yrs and 10 mos d Sun 19 Jan of diptheria.

DJ 15 Feb 1868/Samuel Cooper age 66 d Thurs 6 Feb at the res of his son.

DJ 22 Feb 1868/M 13 Feb at the res of the bride's parents by Rev J. Hough, Caleb C. Wheeler and Miss Mary E. Butler, all of this county.

DJ 29 Feb 1868/M 27 Feb in Hillsboro by Rev G. F. Beavens, George W. Richardson of New York City and Miss Annie M. Redden of this county.

Mrs. Maria L. Emerson wife of Robert R. Emerson age 39 yrs, 6 mos, and 23 das d Sat morning last on 22 Feb.

Mrs. Elizabeth A. Atwell d/o Rev George Heritage d in Denton Tues morning last.

Mrs. Mary E. Hand age 26 yrs, one month and 20 das d 20 Feb.

DJ 14 Mar 1868/M 5th day of the 3rd month 1868 with the consent of Kennett Monthly Meeting Chester County Pa, Nathan Corkran and P. A. Pennock of said county.

Lemmon Catrup infant s/o William T. and Phoebe Ann Slaughter d 5 Mar age 2 mos and 25 das.

Mrs. Margaret Pritchett wife of Edward Pritchett of A d 22 Feb age 78.

Thomas Kelley Willis age 18 yrs and 8 mos d Mon 10 Feb at the res of his father near New Hope.

DJ 21 Mar 1868/William C. Meeds formerly of Greensboro d in Phila Sat 14 Mar age 56.

DJ 28 Mar 1868/George E. Williamson d 19 Feb age 33.

DJ 4 Apr 1868/M at the Presby Church Saulsbury 25 Mar by Rev C. E. Watts, Henry Rawlings of Caroline Co to Ella C. Disharoon of Wicomico Co.

Mrs. Margaret Ann Melvin consort of James Melvin d in Denton Sun afternoon last age 46 yrs, 6 mos and 22 das.

Newspaper Abstracts

DJ 18 Apr 1868/M 7 Apr in Emory M.E. Church by Rev T. Sherlock, Jesse H. T. Hubbard of Easton to Miss Hester A. Fluharty of Balt.

Mrs. Margaret Ann Melvin consort of James Melvin d at her res in Denton 28 Mar age 46 yrs, 6 mos 21 das..."May her two little boys...never lose the influence of her pious instruction..."

DJ 25 Apr 1868/Thomas J. Carter d Wed 22 Apr of heart disease age 40.

DJ 2 May 1868/A little son of Eli Collison aged about 7 or 8 months was killed at the Alms House in this county on Monday last (27 Apr). As the hands were going to work in the field the little boy was placed on the back of a mule to ride. The mule became frightened, put off at full speed, threw the boy when he became entangled in the harness and was dragged some distance. When relieved from this perilous position life was nearly extinct. He died a short time afterwards.

M at the res of the bride's parents Tues morning last by Rev B. F. Benson, Henry C. Fisher and Miss M. Bettie Wilson both of this county.

Rev Henry M. Mason, D. D. of Easton, d of apoplexy 25 Apr.

DJ 9 May 1868/John Bynard Thomas infant s/o Rev B. F. and M. E. Benson d in Denton on Tues 5 May, age 2 mos, 2 weeks and 4 das.

DJ 16 May 1868/J. L. R. Tolson M. D. late U. S. Navy d 1 May age 24.

DJ 30 May 1868/M Tues last (26 May) at the res of the bride's parents by Rev A. Manship assisted by Reverends R. W. Todd and Williams M. Warner, Thurman C. Annabal of Logansport, Indiana and Miss Annie E. d/o Joseph Pearson of this county.

Richard Bishop d in Denton Fri night last (29 May) after a lingering affliction age 40 yrs, 2 mos and 7 das.

William W. Morgan near Hillsborough d 16 May of consumption.

Henry J. Barwick formerly of this county d at his res in Chapel Dist, Talb Co, on 18 May at an advanced age.

DJ 13 Jun 1868/M 28 May at the res of the bride's father by Rev J. B. Merritt, Solomon Pippin of this county and Miss Mary F. d/o Mrs. Isaac Mason of QA Co.

M in Greensborough 4 Jun by Rev W. M. Warner, Benjamin F. Townsend and Miss Mary A. Clarke all of this county.

DJ 4 Jul 1868/On Sun afternoon last (28 Jun) two children of Capt Nathan Corkran res near Dover Bridge were drowned in the Choptank.

M 25 Jun at the res of Richard Ross by Rev William O'Neill, Simeon West and Sarah Straughn all of this county.

Mrs. Sue E. wife of Zeb. Fountain d on the night of the 30th about 19.

Cornelius Comegys, age 71, d in Greensboro 22 Jun.

Mrs. Sara Scott age 68 d at the res of her daughter near Melville 19 Jun. She was a consistent member of the M. E. Church for 50 years.

DJ 18 Jul 1868/M in St Pauls Church Hillsborough 16 Jul by Rev George F. Beaven, Alexander Gadd of Caroline Co and Ella T. Jester of Talb Co.

DJ 25 Jul 1868/ M 15 Jul at the res of James Pippin by Rev William O'Neill, William O'Neill to Martha Pippin, all of this county.

Newspaper Abstracts

Charles H. Hardcastle d in Greensborough 4 Jul, third s/o William E. Hardcastle,age 52

DJ 1 Aug 1868/Robert Dawson, late of this county d 20 Jul near Concord Station Virginia.

George Washington Lee infant s/o John and Isabella H. Thawley d near Glocester Court House Va 18 Jul, age 2 mos and a few das.

"Our community has suddenly been stricken with deep grief on account of the death of our esteemed friend Mrs. Sudie Fountain. Her illness was quite protracted yet she bore it with patient resignation...Two months ago she was in health and vigor..."

DJ 8 Aug 1868/Jacob Morgan infant s/o F. T. and Sara Barton d 20 Jul at Hillsborough age 4 mos and 4 das.

DJ 29 Aug 1868/On Tus night (18 Aug) of last week, in the vicinity of Federalsburg, a young man named Richard Caroll was shot (accidentally) and killed by his brother-in-law a man named Eaton who apparently mistook Caroll for a prowler. Richard Carroll d the following day. The accident occurred at the home of his father-in-law.

"Murder - During the progress of the colored camp at Reeds Wood, William Holmes, barber, was shot (and killed) by Eli Fisher... Wright Satterfield is suspected of being an accomplice in the murder..."

DJ 5 Sep 1868/Eli Collison age about 60 d at the alms house Sun last of rheumatism.

Lewis Edwin s/o Lewis and Sallie Flynn age one year, 11 mos and 23 das d at Hillsboro Sun morning 23 Aug.

Jonathan Tylor age 62 d at his res in Denton Thurs 3 Sep of congestive chill.

DJ 12 Sep 1868/Cathalinda consort of John E. Starkey age 53 d 15 Aug.

Revel Horsey d 9 Sep age 56

Rebecca Carmean age about 20 d 6 Sep in Tuckahoe Neck.

DJ 19 Sep 1868/M 8 Sep at the res of the bride by Rev Marrick, Washington Rowins formerly of this county and Mrs. Sarah E. Dadd of QA Co.

Raymond only child of Philip W. and Annie M. Downes d in Denton 16 Sep at the age of one year and 19 das.

Willie A. Pingrey d near Boonwille 4 Sep of congestive chill age 10 yrs, 4 mos, and 10 das.

DJ 3 Oct 1868/Edward B. Meloney age 58 yrs, 3 mos and 15 das d 24 Sep.

DJ 10 Oct 1868/Archie Cohee d very suddenly at his res Thurs (8 Oct) from congestion of the brain.

On Wed (7 Oct) Mr. A. W. Hines of Greensborough was suddenly attacked by apoplexy and d in a few hrs. Mr. Hines was formerly of Dorch Co but had been engaged in the tailoring business in Greensborough for many yrs.

Mrs. Mary E. Wright wife of D. R. Wright age 43 yrs, 11 mos and 14 das d 2 Aug.

Daniel Edward Wright s/o Daniel R. and Mary E. Wright age 9 mos, 28 das d 2 Aug.

DJ 17 Oct 1868/Bowdle Blades age 46 d at the res of his brother near Bethlehem in the third dist 26 Sep.

Newspaper Abstracts

DJ 31 Oct 1868/M at Piney Neck M.E. Church Thurs 8 Oct by Rev D. C. Ridgeway, William H. Davis and Miss Susie Hopkins, both of QA Co.

DJ 14 Nov 1868/Dr. Andrew Stafford has removed to Crisfield for the purpose of practicing his profession.

Miss Sallie T. Potter age about 65, d/o the late General William Potter of this county d in Balt 4 Nov.

Mrs. Mary Terry wife of Captain Jona. Terry d Sun last (8 Nov) age 60.

Mrs. Mary wid of the late Colin F. Hale d in Kent Co Md 8 Nov, age 65.

Levi Eldridge Passapae d 30 Oct from inflamation of the bowels, age 19 yrs, 5 mos, 16 das.

DJ 5 Dec 1868/M 26 Nov by Rev R. W. Todd, John F. Wilson of New York City and Miss Harriett M. Raymond of this county.

William Williams d at his res Tuckahoe Neck Sun morning last (29 Nov) of chronic rheumatism at age 62.

AU 7 Jan 1869/"Freezed to Death - On Thursday, the 24th of December some parties in Federalsburg prevailed upon William John to go to Greenwood on the Delaware Railroad ten miles distant, lay in a supply of whiskey for Christmas day. The weather was extremely cold and the distance to be traveled on foot. ..." He was found asleep on the return leg of his trip and revived but soon thereafter died.

"The result of a drunken spree - William Parr, an Englishman and engineer at the steam saw mill below Federalsburg, ended his days in a very sad way on Friday night the first inst. (1 Jan). He had come to Mr. John Caroll's public house, in Federalsburg, a few days previous, and engaged board. For about four weeks he had been on a spree, and had brought on himself the delirium tremens - the usual result of such protracted frolics. On the night in question he was in his room and raising his window, he either jumped out or fell out upon the brick pavement below, his head receiving the shock and killing him almost instantly. A coroners' jury was summoned and a verdict rendered in accordance with the above facts."

M in the M.E. Church, Denton on 24 Dec by Rev R. W. Todd, Charles E. Wilson of Easton and Miss Maria M. 2nd d/o John R. Fountain of Denton.

M 22 Dec by Rev John Erwin at the res of the bride's father, Francis T. Jewell and Miss Sarah E. Roe, both of this county.

M 29 Dec by Rev J. W. Hammersley, George W. Camper and Miss Sarah E. Nichols all of this county.

M 30 Dec by Rev J. W. Hammersly, Josiah Barwick and Miss Maggie Jarrell, both of this county.

M at the M.E. Parsonage, Greensborough by Rev William O'Neill, William T. Downes and Miss Annie Willis, all of this county.

M 31 Dec by Rev B. F. Benson, Capt R. R. Emerson and Miss Annie Fisher, both of this county.

M at the res of the bride's father 4 Jan by Rev William M. Warner, H. Kenney and Miss E. Bartie Case, both of Greensborough.

M 29 Dec by Rev William O'Neill, John H. Genn and Miss Susan Carter, both of this county.

Newspaper Abstracts

M 30 Dec by Rev William O'Neill at the res of the bride's uncle, Samuel H. Carter and Miss Anna E. Whitby, both of this county.

Robert May d/o S. Fountain and Anna A. Liden age 2 yrs, 5 mos and 29 das d at Potters Landing on 3 Jan.

Minnie only d/o James W. and Anna C. Davis late of this county d at Union Mo 1 Jan.

DJ 9 Jan 1869/M at the res of the bride's father 6 Dec by Rev B. F. Benson, Isaac D. Anderson and Miss Roxanna Spurry, both of this county.

Mrs. Lucy B. Richardson d at the res of her son-in-law, J. B. Steel, of Denton, on 7 Jan. Mrs. Richardson was the consort of the late Joseph Richardson and d/o General William Potter. She was 75. She is to be buried at the old Lyford burying ground at 10 o'clock this morning.

James Carroll late of this county d near Marshy Hope Bridge 7 Jan, age 76.

AU 14 Jan 1869/M in Chestertown at the res of the bride's mother Tues morning 15 Dec by Rev Daniel Bowers, assisted by Rev J. Thomas Murray, John N. Dood and Miss J. Lucy Smith, all of Chestertown.

AU 21 Jan 1869/M 14 Jan by Rev P. H. Rawlings, Eli Sparklin and Miss Martha Fleetwood, both of this county.

William Frederick, infant s/o Frederick and Sallie Roshy, age 1 mo d in Denton Mon (18 Jan) last.

DJ 23 Jan 1869/William Pinkney White youngest s/o Thomas and Mary F. Melvin, age 2 yrs, 2 mos, 20 das, d at Melville on 13 Jan.

AU 28 Jan 1869/M 13 Jan by Rev E. Stubbs, William J. Comegys of this county and Miss Mary A. Porter of Kent Co Md.

Mrs. Sarah Matilda wife of John Minner near Denton d Fri last 22 Jan, age 26.

Miss Mary Dill near Punch Hall d Fri last (22 Jan) age 21.

Mrs. Chaney Hubbard d near Piney Grove Sat last 23 Jan at an advanced age.

Mrs. Sara Turner age about 60 d at her res in Harmony Wed 20 Jan.

DJ 30 Jan 1869/M 27 Jan by Rev J. W. Hammersly, Charles W. Aringdale of Talb Co and Miss Louisa E. Chaffinch of Caroline Co.

Elizabeth Sparklin wife of Thomas Sparklin d at her res in Tuckahoe Neck 21 Jan age 65.

AU 4 Feb 1869/Near Greensborough Mrs. Massey wife of James Massey d Mon last (1 Feb) age about 30.

DJ 6 Feb 1869/M 27 Jan by Rev J. W. Hammersly, James H. Horsey and Miss Josephine Wright, both of this county.

William Smith s/o Henry H. Smith d in Tuckahoe Neck 4 Feb of consumption, age about 21.

AU 11 Feb 1869/M 28 Jan by Rev W. Kenney, D. D., John E. Sewell and Miss Annie E. d/o Henry Corkran, all of Easton.

William Baker d at his res near Denton 4 Feb age 43.

AU 18 Feb 1869/M 10 Feb by Rev R. W. Todd, George Cohee and Miss Rebecca E. Williamson, all of this county.

Newspaper Abstracts

AU 25 Feb 1869/M Wed 17 Feb at Salem M. E. Church by Rev Merrill, John W. Fletcher and Miss Sussie Higgins, all of Dorch Co.

William Horsey s/o John H. Horsey, age about 20, d Sun morning last. (21 Feb)

Robert Faulkner, age about 50, d at his res in Tuckahoe Neck Sat last (20 Feb).

Mrs. Jane Bradley d at her res near Vernon Del 18 Feb, age 79.

Annie A. d/o Alfred and Lavenia E. Kemp d 10 Feb age 3 yrs, 11 mos, 15 das.

Charles Hill infant s/o Rev J. W. and Anna Hammersly d in Denton Fri last. (19Feb) age 11 mos.

Mrs. Fannie Hopkins wife of Samuel T. Hopkins d in Easton Sun night 21 Feb after a few hours illness, age 39.

DJ 27 Feb 1869/Elisha Corkran age 76 yrs, 8 mos, 16 das, d in New Hope in this county 2 Jan.

AU 4 Mar 1869/"A little child of a colored man named Matthews residing on Mr. Joseph Pearson's farm near Denton was burned to death on Sunday last (28 Feb)." Her clothes caught fire from the fireplace. She was about 5 yrs old.

M 18 Feb by Rev William R. McFarlane at Boonville, Robert C. Eaton and Miss A. V. Williamson, both of this county.

M at the res of the bride's father James Pippin on Sun (28 Feb) by Rev William R. McFarlane, William T. Swann and Miss Mahala A. Pippin, both of this county.

Mary E. Adams, colored, d at her father's res near Preston, age 26 yrs, 4 mos, and 8 das.

AU 11 Mar 1869/M 9 Feb by Rev William O'Neill, William Quimby of Talb Co and Miss Annie E. Orrell of this county.

M by Rev William O'Neill 24 Feb, Thomas Coleman of QA Co and Miss Louisa Wells of this county.

Mr. F. W. Ridgely d 8 Mar, age 41.

Josephine R. youngest child of the late Josiah Jump d 4 Mar, age 2 yrs, 4 mos.

Mrs. Margaret Horsey wife of Jacob Horsey d 4 Mar of consumption, age about 25. She was the d/o Tilghman Nuttle.

AU 25 Mar 1869/M 11 Mar by Rev R. C. Allison, John E. Starkey and Miss Mary E. Mullican, both of Caroline Co.

William W. Medford d at his res near Denton Fri morning last (19 Mar) age 68.

AU 1 Apr 1869/M in Greensborough 29 Mar by Rev Richard Chambers, Charles H. Manship and Miss Margaret Ellen Hobbs, both of this county.

M in Wilmington Del 22 Mar by Rev James Esgate, William H. Stafford and Mrs. M. Emma Gootee, both of this county.

Mrs. Rebecca A. Gouty d in Denton Mon morning last (29 Mar) age 81.

AU 8 Apr 1869/James E. Bryan d near Denton Sun morning last (4 Apr) age 23.

AU 8 Apr 1869/Willie s/o James S. and Sallie Rickards d Tues last (6 Apr) age 6.

Sarah C. Pool wife of James H. Pool d near Easton Tues 23 Mar, age 24 yrs, 6 mos and 24 das. after an illness of about 12 hrs.

Newspapers Abstracts

AU 17 Apr 1869/James E. Blackiston d at his res in Kent Co Md 30 Mar of paralysis, age 60.

AU 29 Apr 1869/Samuel S. Hitch, age 23 yrs and 5 mos, d at the res of Matthew Chilton on Fri evening last (23 Apr) of consumption.

John Grant s/o Joshua and Mary W. Seward age 4 yrs and 18 das d 14 Apr.
Mrs. Ann Hubbard d Fri last (23 Apr) age about 60.

AU 6 May 1869/"Mr. Samuel H. Carter, son of Samuel M. Carter Esq. died very suddenly at his residence on Rev. R. W. Todd's farm near this town on Friday morning last (30 Apr) ... His disease seems to have been colic in its most virulent form. He was in the prime of life and has been married but a few months..."

Samuel H. Carter, age about 22, d at his res near Denton 26 Apr after an illness of a few hours.

AU 13 May 1869/Mrs. Sarah A. Newman d near Royal Oak 27 Apr age 44.

AU 20 May 1869/Hubert B. s/o Captain D. E. and Mary E. Somers d Thurs evening last (13 May), age 7.

James Butler d near Smithville Tues of last week (11 May) age 88.

Miss Louisa Peters d 13 May, age about 21.

Ezekiel Smith d Sun last (16 May) at his res in first dist.

Mrs. Melvin wife of Isaac Melvin of the firs dist d Sun last (16 May).

AU 3 Jun 1869/"Nelse Allen a colored man much advanced in years was found dead in the woods Friday last (28 May) by John Rich near Burrsville. He had not been seen since the Monday previous... Generally appeared to have been the result of natural causes."

AU 3 Jun 1869/M 27 May by Rev R. W. Todd, James B. Dukes and Miss Mary E. McCormic.

AU 10 Jun 1869/William Hardcastle d very suddenly at the res of his father in the first dist Wed morning last (9 Jun), age about 50.

Lavinia Jarrel wife of Thomas Jarrell d Mon week (31 May) at her res, age about 60.

AU 17 Jun 1869/A son of William Williams res near Marydel was drowned in the mill pond near Marydel on Sun morning (13 Jun), age about 18 yrs old.

M 15 Jun at Concord M.E. Church by Rev R. W. Todd, Garey H. Leaverton of Kent Co Md and Miss Mary E. Purt of this county.

Mrs. Ann S. Griffith d Tues morning last (15 Jun) at the res of her son-in-law J. Boon Dukes near Denton, age 52. Mrs Griffith was the relict of the late Charles A. Griffith. She is to be buried at Griffith Farm Thurs.

M Sun evening last (20 Jun) by Rev R. W. Todd, Thomas E. Sharp of Sussex Co Del and Miss Martha P. Sullivan of this county.

Thomas B. Quigley d in Felton Del 17 Jun of consumption, age about 30.

AU 1 Jul 1869/Stephen Colescott d 23 Jun at his res near Denton of paralysis, age 71.

Rev Gabriel Friend d at his res near Bethlehem 19 Jun, age 69.

Newspaper Abstracts

AU 8 Jul 1869/Capt Henry Straughn d at his res near Ruthsburg Fri last (2 Jul) age about 65.

Earle Tildon, infant child of Henry A. and Fannie Sparks, d in Denton Fri last (2 Jul) age 2 mos, 2 weeks and 4 das.

AU 15 Jul 1869/"Thomas Holliday, a colored man residing near Upper Hunting Creek, a few days ago accidently killed one of his children by letting a log of wood fall endwise upon it..."

AU 22 Jul 69/Martha wife of Robert H. Colescott d in Talb Co 11 Jul of consumption, age 24.

DJ 24 Jul 69/The funeral of the late William W. Medford will be preached at Wesley's Sun 1 Aug by Rev J. W. Hammersly at 10 o'clock A. M.

Mrs. Hannah Whitesides, age 76, d at the res of her son near Fowling Creek 11 Jul after a long and severe illness "borne with Christian fortitude."

AU 29 Jul 69/"A party of colored men went into the river on Mr. John D. Williams shore on Saturday evening last (24 Jul) for the purpose of bathing when one of the number, William H. Moloch drowned..." He is to be interred in the colored people's burial ground.

Lewis Merce s/o Lewis C. Green d Sat last (24 Jul) of dysentery, age 4 yrs, 2 mos and 4 das.

DJ 31 Jul 69/Daniel Spahr formerly of Pennsylvania but who has been res in Greensborough for some time d very suddenly on the afternoon of Fri of last week (23 Jul). He was engaged in assisting in the running of a car on the switch when he expired.

AU 5 Aug 69/"On Saturday morning last the existence of a son of Mr. Moses F. Towns was terminated quite abruptly ... attacked by a sudden fit and died..."

Miss Henrietta Swann age about 15 d Thurs last (29 Jul).

AU 12 Aug 69/Joseph Stafford age about 22 d Thurs night last (5 Aug) of consumption.

Mrs. Annie C. "beloved companion" of J. W. Davis and d/o Rev E. Davis of the Wilmington Conference d in Marshfield Mo 3 Aug after an illness of 12 weeks.

Mrs. Nixie E. wife of John H. Ross and d/o William Gullett of this county d in Cambridge 4 Aug, age 26.

AU 26 Aug 1869/Joseph Pearson d at the res of his father-in-law Fri last (20 Aug) of typhoid fever, age 43, after a short illness. He was a member of the M.E. Church in Denton. His remains were interred at Milton Del.

Mary Corine, third d/o John H. and Nixie E. Ross, age 7 mos and 17 das, d 14 Aug.

AU 9 Sep 1869/Lizzie Roberta only child of J. Marion and Lizzie S. Emerson d at the res of Mrs. J. Stewart in Gloucester Co, N.J. Mon 6 Sep, age 1 yr, 1 month, 23 das.

Abram Y. Collins d at his res Sun last (5 Sep) age 48.

AU 16 Sep 1869/M at the res of the bride's mother 9 Sep by Rev William S. Barnert, James A. Fountain of Denton and Miss Anna B. Stewart of Gloucester Co, N.J.

Philip Alvon only child of Philip W. and Anna H. Downes d in Denton 9 Sep, age 8 mos and 22 das.

Newspaper Abstracts

AU 23 Sep 1869/M 16 Sep by Rev J. M. McCarter, John Leigh and Miss Celia Turner, all of the third dist Caroline Co.

AU 7 Oct 1869/M at the Greensborough M.E. Parsonage 23 Sep by Rev W. B. Gregg, Ed. B. Mitchell and Miss Ellen E. Porter, all of this county.

AU 14 Oct 1869/Thomas P. s/o John W. Christopher, age 20 yrs, 4 mos and 21 das, d at the res of his father in Kent Co Del.

M 2 Oct by Rev Eliott, Charles B. Worrell M.D. of Federalsburg and Miss Carrie Auerbacher of Phila.

M 5 Oct by Rev R. W. Todd, George H. Hollis and Miss Sallie A. Stayton, both of Sussex Co Del.

AU 21 Oct 1869/Thomas Atkinson d 12 Oct at his res in Tuckahoe Neck, age 70.

AU 28 Oct 1869/M 19 Oct by Rev Dr. Lavin at St. Peters Church, Eugene W. Humphreys to Miss M. Josephine Tarr d/o J. Hopkins Tarr, all of Salisbury Md.

AU 11 Nov 1869/M 3 Nov by Rev J. W. Hammersly, John W. Lockerman and Miss Eliza Ross, both of this county.

AU 18 Nov 1869/"The terrible burning of the wife of Luff Lewis has resulted in death."

"James H. Willoughby son of Captain Daniel Willoughby of this county fell overboard from the schooner Lydia A. Hughlett, Captain Corkran, when off Point No Point in the Chesapeake on Monday the first instant and was drowned before assistance could reach him."

AU 25 Nov 1869/"John D. Kemp has abandoned the practice of law and will lead a farmers life upon Kent Island."

"Dr. J. A. McLean of Norwalk Connecticut purchaser of the Zook property has removed there with his family. His son also a physician has come down with him."

M Thurs last (18 Nov) in Balt, William Edgar Addison of that city and Miss Sallie Postlethwaite of Denton.

AU 2 Dec 1869/Margaret Winnifred d/o Thomas and Mary Ellen Numbers d Kent Co Md 26 Nov, age 3.

AU 9 Dec 1869/Mrs. Margret A. Gullet consort of Albert G. Gullet d in Phila 6 Dec, age 45. Her funeral is to be held in the M.E. Church Denton at 10 O'clock today.

Emma G. 2nd d/o Thomas N. and Emily A. Gould d in Balt 3 Dec of typhoid fever.

Mrs. E. Bartie Kenney wife of D. H. Kenney and d/o Thomas D. and Eliza A. Case d 2 Dec age 22 yrs, 1 month and 16 das.

M 1 Dec by Rev Esgate, John W. Stevens and Miss Lusetta V. Marble, both of this county.

M 24 Nov by Rev J. W. Hammersley, Thomas A. Melvin of Missouri and Miss Celia Ellen Noble of this county.

M 15 Nov at the res of the bride's father near Key Port, N.J. by the Rev Hewitt, W. Edgar Harris of this county to Miss Annie B. Murphy.

M in Phila 30 Nov by Rev R. W. Todd assisted by Rev Dr. Alday, Joseph C. McBride of Camden Del and Miss Emma W. Todd of Denton.

AU 16 Dec 1869/M 9 Dec by Rev R. W. Todd, Owen C. Blades and Miss Rhoda Fountain, all of this county.

M Tues last (14 Dec) at the bride's res by Rev J. W. Hammersley, James Melvin and Mrs. Margaret H. Jump, both of this county.

Miss Kate Pearson, age about 25, d at Ridgely Fri last (10 Dec).

AU 6 Jan 1870/"Still at large - Cyrus Stack, the murderer of Benjamin Rhodes at Crotchers Ferry, recently, is still at large, having eluded the officers of the law..."

M 3 Jan by Rev R. W. Todd, Wesley Smith and Miss Almira Taylor, all of this county.

M at the res of the bride 30 Dec, Kelly Gootee and Miss Rachael S. W. Cox, both of Balt.

M 4 Jan by Rev J. W. Hammersley, Phillip B. Noble and Mrs. Mary Willemina Breeding, both of this county.

M at the res of Noah Patrick 23 Dec by Rev William R. McFarlane, Daniel Montague of Kent Co Del and Susan K. Burt of this county.

Mrs. Samuel Lang d at Potters Landing 18 Dec after a lingering illness of six months.

Miss Sallie J. Johnson d 18 Dec age 26 yrs, 6 mos and 8 das.

Minos Adams d near Federalsburg 30 Dec age 93 yrs, 7 mos and 29 das.

Mrs. Anna Connolly wife of William Connolly Jr d 27 Dec near Hillsboro, age 28.

AU 6 Jan 1870/Capt E. C. Brown d at the res of Foster Green 27 Dec, age 30 yrs, 11 mos, and 27 das.

AU 13 Jan 1870/"Enoch Ross a very industrious and worthy colored citizen of this district died at his residence on Monday night week (3 Jan). By his accumulating a sufficiency to live comfortably upon and had his life been prolonged to a sufficient length we doubt not that he would have been an honor and an ornament to his race...(He) held a position of high esteem.

Thomas P. Simpson, age 46, d in Denton 6 Jan.

AU 27 Jan 1870/M 3 Jan by Rev J. W. Hammersley, Robert D. Windsor and Isabella Price, both of this county.

M 19 Jan by Rev J. W. Hammersley, Levi D. Roe and Miss Frances Camper, both of this county.

M at Marydell 13 Jan by Rev William R. McFarlane, Daniel Hayden and Miss Miriam Pippin, both of this county.

J. B. Calloway d at his res in Tuckahoe Neck Mon last (24 Jan).

AU 3 Feb 1870/M at the M.E. Parsonage Greensborough 27 Jan by Rev W. B. Gregg, Charles W. Smith and Miss Laura E. Brown, all of this county.

Francis, infant s/o W. S. and A. W. Ridgely, d 26 Jan of whooping cough, age 5 week and 4 das.

Mrs Elizabeth L. Lacy relict of the late Dr. George W. Lacy of this county d in Centreville Sun week (23 Jan).

AU 10 Feb 1870/M 27 Jan by Rev Baldwin, Charles H. Whitby and Miss Annie E. d/o Edgar Plummer, all of this county.

Washington Rowlins d at his res Talb Co 6 Feb, age about 56.

AU 17 Feb 1870/Federalsburg item - Jacob Francis s/o Clement Sullivan "gentle, amiable and pleasant youth of 15 years' d 9 Feb after two yrs of ill health.

AU 17 Feb 1870/Martha E. infant d/o Samuel E. and Martha E. Miller d 14 Feb age 7 mos.

AU 23 Feb 1870/Joseph Brooks formerly of New York state but at the time of his death res on his farm lately purchased from Charles A. Dunning d very suddenly from Heart disease Sun last (23 Feb), age 47.

Mr. Ridgely d 16 Feb.

Margaret A. wife of Peter Draper d 16 Feb, age 34.

Susie infant child of J. B. and Hettie Williams d 16 Feb, age 14 mos.

AU 3 Mar 1870/M at Pippin's M.E. Church 22 Feb by Rev W. B. Gregg, William H. Vane and Miss Laura V. Lane, both of this county.

William Walter Hoff d 23 Feb, age about 44.

James T. Richardson d Mon night (28 Feb) last, age about 45.

AU 10 Mar 1870/"Frank Hubbard a young lad, age about 14 years, and brother of William J. Hubbard residing at Denton Bridge died on Saturday last (5 Mar) from Hydrophobia. Sometime during last summer he was bitten by a mad dog, but the effects of the bite did not become apparent until lately. We learn that he had 29 fits before death relieved him of his sufferings."

Seward an aged citizen of Greensborough d very suddenly on the night of 27 Feb of a paralytic stroke. It came on at 6 P.M. and he d at 3 o'clock on the following morning. He was said to be the greatest walker in Caroline Co.

Mrs. Mary Hubbard wife of Thomas Hubbard, age about 90, d 7 Mar.

Mrs. Sarah L. wife of John H. Emerson, age 53, d in Denton Tues morning last of consumption.

William Newlee a citizen of the first dist has moved to Indiana, there to see a competency for himself and family.

William Quimby who several years ago taught singing schools in the upper part of this county where he made many friends, d at Annapolis Sunday (6 Mar).

AU 24 Mar 1870/"...wife of Rev William McFarlane of the M.E. Conference, late of Halltown but at this time visiting her parents at Duck Creek rose from her bed...wandered off in the direction of Duck Creek...(She was) found about 3 o'clock Thursday morning thinly clad lying against a log in Denny's mill race in a state of unconsciousness and her lower limbs frozen to the bone... it is thought (she) cannot recover."

AU 31 Mar 1870/On Thurs morning the 24th Levin Wright d at his res in Bethlehem. His funeral Sat was largely attended. ...much esteemed by his numerous friends and acquaintances who will long remember the years he spent in their midst and feel the pain of separation. He leaves 10 children and a widow to mourn his loss, who have the sympathy of all who are acquainted with them."

"Henderson item - Western fever- W. J. Connelly, A. Miller, David Straughn, John Laws Jr, John McDonald, James A. Shaw, wife and three children. A party of 12 or 15 or more are to start next Monday - They will settle in the states of Indiana, Illinois, Iowa, Missouri and Kansas."

Newspaper Abstracts

M at Friendship, New York, 10 Mar at the res of the bride's mother by Rev
Jackson, Charles F. Maclary of Clayton Del to Miss Mary J. Calkins.

AU 7 Apr 1870/David Williams an aged citizen res on the edge of Delaware near
Johnsons Crossroads d very suddenly Fri last (1 Apr). His sickness was only
of about 10 minutes duration.

Miss Jane Wood age 15 d at the res of John H. Horsey Sun night last(3 Apr).

John Walter s/o Alfred and Lavinia E. Kemp d at Potters Landing 3 Mar age
9 mos and 5 das.

AU 13 Apr 1870/Daniel T. Bowdle d at his res Thurs last (7 Apr) of consumption,
age about 45 yrs.

William Twiford s/o Artemus Smith deceased, d 19 Mar of pneumonia, age 18 yrs,
2 mos and 16 das.

AU 28 Apr 1870/An old and highly esteemed colored man, Solomon Grinnage d
strickened with an apoplectic fit. He was engaged in field work at the time.
He d within 4 hours after the seizure.

The wife of Mr. ___ Shaeffer of the second dist "eloped with a man named
Joseph Baird. Baird is a carpenter who loves his liquor..."

"First dist item - William R. Hynson who went west for his health informs me
that he has had another severe Hemorrhage and fears that his race is nearly
run.... an exemplary young man."

AU 19 May 1870/John Morgan s/o John Morgan d suddenly at the almshouse a few
days ago. He was sitting upright in a chair and fell back without a struggle.
His disease was the consumption. He had been an inmate of the institution but
a short time.

AU 26 May 1870/M 12 May by Rev T. J. Kenny, W. H. Alburger and Miss Hattie W.
Noble, both of Federalsburg.

S. M. Raymond s/o Capt T. M. Raymond of this county d suddenly in New Haven
Ct 13 May.

AU 9 Jun 1870/John W. Clark of Tuckahoe Neck has purchased a farm in Michigan.

M 10 May at the res of the bride's father by Rev George McKee, Rev Alex
Manship of the St. Louis Annual Conference and Miss Melinda J. Ing of
Knobnoster Mo.

AU 23 Jun 1870/M in Phila 15 Jun by Rev Paxon, Mr. W. T. A. Lockerman and Miss
Emily Blades, d/o the late Isaiah C. Blades, both of this county.

Daniel Todd d 20 Jun at his res near Preston at an advanced age.

John W. Atkinson, age about 35, d on the morning of 22 Jun of consumption.

AU 30 Jun 1870/Marion Clinton s/o J. Marion and Lizzie S. Emerson, age 7 mos
and 24 das d in Denton on the morning of 24 Jun.

Celona only child of Levin W. and Sallie A. Williams, age 6 mos and 28 das d
9 Jun.

AU 14 Jul 1870/Horace Lee s/o George W. and Annie M. Richardson, age 6 mos and
24 das d 7 Jul of cholera infantum.

Willie Milton s/o Francis S. and Lizzie Todd d at Harmony 11 Jul, age 8 mos and
13 das.

AU 21 Jul 1870/William Frank Gadd d 15 Jul at his res near Hillsboro of consumption, age 35 yrs, 7 mos and 17 das.

Joseph K. C. Bryant s/o J. W. and S. H. Bryant, age 9 mos and 12 das d Sat 16 Jul.

Thomas Kennedy s/o Thomas and Annie M. West d of dysentery 29 Jun, age 7 yrs, 7 mos and 7 das.

AU 28 Jul 1870/M at the M. P. Church Centerville 20 Jul, John T. Hand, editor of the "Maryland Citizen" and Miss Maggie Harper, both of Centreville.

Mrs. Mary B. Dunning relict of the late Samuel d at the res of her son Charles A. Dunning Sun last (24 Jul) age 68.

William Thomas s/o Calvin Q. and Henrietta McClayland d at Potters Landing 20 Jul, age 2 yrs, 5 mos and 17 das.

Mary Eliza infant d/o Samuel H. and Mary E. Plummer d near Easton 19 Jul age 10 mos and 23 das.

AU 4 Aug 1870/Mrs. Jane Pippin wife of James Pippin d 30 Jun of consumption age 58.

J. Howard s/o J. H. and N. Mason d 8 Jul, age 1 yr, 10 mos and 2 das.

AU 11 Aug 1870/Florence Alberta only d/o Lewis and Sallie Flynn, age 4 mos and 9 das d in Easton 31 Jul.

AU 18 Aug 1870/Laura Grant d/o Peter and Margaret Ann Draper d 23 Jul age 11 mos and 21 das.

Elizabeth Roberta d/o Joshua and Mary W. Seward d 29 Jul, age 11 mos and 17 das.

AU 1 Sep 1870/Anna W. age 9 mos and 20 das d 11 Aug and Alphonsa age 9 mos and 26 das d 17 Aug, daughters of Richard C. and Eliza A. Jones in Greensborough.

Michael Connolly, age about 70 yrs d at his res near Chestnut Wood schoolhouse 28 Aug.

AU 8 Sep 1870/M 1 Sep at the res of Rev J. L. Kenney near New Hope by Rev James T. Kenney, Thomas H. Nichols to Miss Emily Edgell, both of this county.

George T. Burgess former sheriff of QA Co d at his res in Church Hill Sun 28 Aug age about 44.

Colonel William B. Paca d at Wye Hall, QA Co Wed 31 Aug, age 70.

AU 15 Sep 1870/M in the parlor of Wilson Hotel by Rev Charles P. Straughn 8 Sep, Michael R. Lockerman and Miss Sarah Emma Todd, both of this county.

James R. Nichols, age 61, d 30 Aug.

AU 23 Sep 1870/Joseph M. Satterthwaite of Denton started for Kansas yesterday morning. He expects to make that state his foster home.

M 15 Sep at Hillsborough M.E. Parsonage by Rev William R. McFarlane, William H. Smithers and Miss Josephine Saxton, both of Talb Co.

AU 29 Sep 1870/M 22 Sep by Rev W. R. McFarlane, Samuel Collins and Miss Carrie Daffin, both of Talb Co.

M at Hillsboro 27 Sep by Rev George F. Beaven, A. J. Gadd and Mrs. Lizzie H. Morgan.

AU 6 Oct 1870/M at the res of William K. Boyle, Balt, Thurs 22 Sep by Rev William K. Boyle, Levi Pippin to Miss Clara McConner, both of QA Co.

Kelly oldest s/o Dr. E. E. and Elizabeth Atkinson d 27 Sep, age 13.

AU 13 Oct 1870/M by Hon. Daniel M. Fox, Mayor of the city of Phila, at his res Thurs evening last 6 Oct, J. H. Emerson and Miss Rebecca A. Dunning, both of Denton.

AU 20 Oct 1870/M at St. Paul's Church Centreville Thurs morning 6 Oct by Rev A. S. Smith, William W. Busteed, editor of the Centreville Observer, to Miss Pattie Vickers youngest d/o the late Samuel Vickers of QA Co.

M at Seaford Del by W. B. Gregg, John C. Mills and Miss Sara E. Willy, all of Sussex Co Del.

M 13 Oct at Seaford Del by W. B. Gregg, James A. Harris and Miss Ruth H. Adams from near Bridgeville Del.

AU 27 Oct 1870/George eldest s/o George W. and Margaret Taylor, age 8 yrs, d near Centreville 15 Oct.

Rev T. J. Quigley, D. D., d at his res in Laurel Del 19 Oct.

AU 10 Nov 1870/George s/o Caleb Satterfield, colored, was drowned Sat afternoon last (5 Nov) in the Choptank, near the Stakes by falling overboard from a boat in which he was crossing the river, age about 10 yrs.

AU 17 Nov 1870/M Thurs last (10 Nov) at the M.E. Church in Denton by Rev R. W. Todd, William A. G. Gullett formerly editor of the Denton Journal and Miss Corine Saulsbury d/o the late J. R. T. Saulsbury.

M at the res of the bride's father 3 Nov by Rev W. M. Warner, Thomas Jarrell and Miss Mary Hubbard d/o Ennalls Hubbard.

M 13 Oct in Phila by Rev J. M. Wheeler, Ovid E. Rochester and Miss Annie A. d/o John R. Fountain of Denton.

Henry Edgar youngest s/o Henry Corkran, age 10 yrs, 9 mos and 1 day, d at Jacksonville, Fla 3 Nov.

AU 24 Nov 1870/Rev John F. Meredith born in this county is at present occupying a pulpit in Reading Pa.

"On Thursday morning (17 Nov) a cart heavily loaded with wood ran over the head of a little (son of) John Baynard, sawyer at Satterfield and Moores Mill near Greensborough..." He lived only a few hours after the accident.

John Talbot age 66 d at Hillsborough 16 Nov.

AU 1 Dec 1870/Mrs. Ann Russom wife of John H. Russom d in Greensborough 22 Nov age 66.

AU 8 Dec 1870/Robert E. Hardcastle of the first dist d Sat (3 Dec) aged about 55. He was buried with Masonic honors on Mon.

Marcey Fountain formerly of this county has been appointed an auctioneer in Balt City by Governor Bowie.

The tenth anniversary of the marriage of Mr. and Mrs. John Wilson res near Federalsburg was celebrated 21 Nov.

M in Balt 1 Dec by Rev E. F. Dashiel assisted by Rev G. F. Beavon, Charles Stevens of Denton and Miss Sue E. Kemp of Talb Co.

Newspaper Abstracts

AU 15 Dec 1870/M in Easton 1 Dec by Rev J. L. Shipley, L. M. Robinson of Caroline Co and Miss Marietta Lofton of Talb.

M at the res of the bride's father 14 Dec, J. W. Kerr of Denton and Miss Amanda C. Sisk d/o William Sisk of Preston.

Mrs. Sarah Roe late of Caroline Co age 59 d 20 Nov near Easton.

AU 19 Jan 1871/The Richmond papers announced the death there of Capt Henry Davis, city grain measurer - For the past 42 yrs Mr. Davis has been a citizen of Richmond but was born and spent his earlier life in this county.

AU 26 Jan 1871/"Mr. Owen Morgan and old and respected citizen of Caroline County d very suddenly on Thursday morning last of heart disease..." He d at his res on the morning of 19 Jan, age about 72.

M 11 Jan by Rev E. H. Hynson, William H. Hollis and Miss Fannie E. Cox, both of Preston.

M 19 Jan by Rev George F. Beavon, Edward C. Carter and Miss Annie L. Downes, all of this county.

M 5 Jan by Rev W. B. Gregg, Henry M. Pool of this county and Miss Fannie Sullivan of Dorch Co.

M at the res of Isaac M. Fisher by Rev W. B. Gregg, Henry L. Philips and Miss Laura Reynolds, all of Seaford Del.

AU 2 Feb 1871/M 24 Jan, Mr. W. W. Medford and Miss Jan Wyatt, both of this county.

M 25 Jan by Rev W. G. Holmes, Silas Nichols and Miss Mary E. Blades, both of this county.

Harry s/o Daniel and Harriett Fields d 30 Jan age 2 yrs, 9 mos.

Joseph s/o Jonathan T. and Eliza Noble d Fri last (21 Jan) in Sussex Co Del age 16.

M 30 Jan by Rev W. G. Holmes, William Burkegt and Miss Rosa Koon, both of this county.

M 12 Jan by Rev W. G. Holmes, Henry F. Collins and Miss Martha Sparklin, both of this county.

M at the M.E. Church Denton 25 Jan by Rev J. W. Hammersly, W. H. Blackiston and Miss Lida Horsey, both of Denton.

AU 9 Feb 1871/M in Greensborough 2 Feb by Rev C. F. Sheppard, Dr. T. J. Smithers of Denton and Miss Sue Roe of Greensborough.

Mrs. James Saulsbury d near Hillsborough Fri morning last (3 Feb) of Pneumonia age 62 yrs, 5 mos and 6 das.

AU 16 Feb 1871/M at the res of the bride's parents in Reeds Creek Neck on 2 Feb by Rev T. D. Valliant, Mr. F. M. Fish of Greensborough and Miss H. Augusta Anthony of QA Co.

Agnes Josephine infant d/o J. Boon and Lou Dukes d Fri last (10 Feb) age 5 mos.

AU 23 Feb 1871/Collins Tatman formerly of Caroline Co d in Wilmington 11 Feb.

Maria Bell consort of the late Rev John Bell d in Martinsburg W. Va 13 Feb, age 78.

Newspaper Abstracts

AU 2 Mar 1871/M at St. Joseph's Church Talb Co 21 Feb by Rev Falter Meurer, William F. Griffith of Del and Miss Marian Wilson d/o William H. Wilson, formerly of Denton.

Mrs. Ellen M. consort of Samuel H. Horsey d Tues afternoon last (28 Feb), age 47.

AU 9 Mar 1871/M 2 Mar by Rev J. W. Hammersley, W. Frank Towers to Miss Manie B. Garey, both of this county.

M 2 Mar by Rev J. W. Hammersley, James B. Cohee to Mrs. Mahala Cohee, both of this county.

Nehemiah Fountain d at his res in Denton Wed last (1 Mar), age 79.

Willis S. youngest child of Horace H. and Ann Boynton Lockwood d at Potters Landing 14 Feb, age 2 yrs and 2 mos.

AU 16 Mar 1871/M 16 Jan at the res of Warner R. Busteed in Phila, Eli S. Smith of Del and Miss Susan J. Gullett of Caroline Co.

William G. Nicholson d in Denton Sat morning last (11 Mar) of consumption, age 47.

AU 23 Mar 1871/Eugene Hubbard, the crushing of whose leg resulted in lock jaw, d from the effects of it.

AU 30 Mar 1871/Charley Sharp, a colored boy in the employ of William E. Pritchett near Preston died. (apparently from lock jaw)

M 19 Feb by Rev R. W. Todd, Frank A. Mobray of Balt City and Miss Dora Mobray of Federalsburg.

Miss Rebecca Sparklin d/o Daniel Sparklin d 23 Mar, age 23.

AU 6 Apr 1871/A child of Thomas Lister d suddenly of congestion of the brain Wed of last week (29 Mar).

"Still West Bound - The western fever is still raging in the upp district and another part left for the West on Monday. The party consisted of Mr. Thomas Clendenning, Mr. Augustus Miller and family, Mr. John Jones and Mr. John C. Jones. These parties intend to settle in Illinois. Mr. John Wyth and family left a few weeks ago. He also went to Illinois."

"More Overland Emigrants - Emigrants continue to arrive at Ridgely. Mr. W. Patmor arrived on Tuesday week with a two-horse team from Tiuga County New York, about 400 miles. On 25 March Mr. Hann and family from Luzerne County Pennsylvania arrived and ... Mr. L. S. Pratt of Brownsville New York arrived the same day."

AU 4 May 1871/"Dr. Rousett one of the oldest citizen of this county died at his residence in Greensborough on Friday morning last (28 Apr)... He removed to this county in 1820. He was in the battle of Waterloo under Wellington... located at Greensborough immediately upon arrival in this county..."

AU 11 May 1871/M 6 Apr by Rev C. F. Sheppard, Frederick J. King of Phila and Miss Cecillia Stack of Greensborough.

M Thurs evening last (4 May) by Rev S. T. Gardner, John Wyatt and Miss Anna M. Butler d/o Moses Butler, both of this county.

Mrs. Elizabeth Andrew d Sun last (7 May) age 82.

AU 18 May 1871/Eddie, a six-year old s/o John R. Wright living near Preston was killed on Tues afternoon of last week (9 May) by being run over by an ox cart.

Newspaper Abstracts

AU 25 May 1871/"Mr. Charles Peters residing below Andersontown fell from his dearborn and broke his neck. He had been to one of Delaware shores after trout and was returning home under the influence of liquor... died before assistance reached him..."

M Thurs last (18 May by Rev S. T. Gardner, Thomas E. Evans and Miss Mollie E. Clark, both of this county.

AU 1 Jun 1871/Ennalls Breeding age about 45 d Mon night last (29 May) of consumption.

AU 15 Jun 1871/M in Lynn Mass 1 Jun by Rev Edward L. Drown, Hon. Henry H. Goldsborough of Easton and Miss Kate H. Caldwell of Boston.

M 7 Jun at the res of William Wilkinson by Rev G. F. Beaven, George W. Wilson of Talb Co and Miss Annie D. Greenley of this county.

Amanda Frances only d/o John and Elizabeth Beachamp d 12 Jun age 2 yrs, 9 mos, and 29 das.

AU 22 Jun 1871/Jacob Whitaker formerly a citizen of this county but from several yrs past a res of Kent Co Del d at his res in Farmington on 15 Jun. ...from a malignant form of billious dysentery, age 61. He leaves a wife and six children.

Robert Nichols, age about 70, d at his res near Friendship.

Mrs. Silas Nichols d at the res of her husband near New Hope, age about 50 yrs.

Kate only child of Philip F. and Margaret Fletcher d in Denton Tues last (20 Jun), age 4 mos and 6 das.

AU 29 Jun 1871/M at the M.E. Parsonage of Caroline Circuit 26 Jun by Rev William H. Lane, William H. Biddel to Anna C. Poor, both of this county.

Charles Willis d at his res in Federalsburg Sun evening 11 Jun, age 72.

Arlington youngest child of William P. and Mary F. Sparks d 17 Jun age 4 mos and 7 das.

AU 13 Jul 1871/M 15 Jun by Rev James Rich, Alexander S. Griffith to Miss Rebecca Baker, both of this county.

Lizzie S. wife of J. Marion Emerson editor of American Union d at the res of her mother in Gloucester Co N.J. age 24 yrs, 8 mos and 16 das.

White Barwick d Tue 29 Jun at the residence of Mr. Billips near Upper Hunting Creek age 64.

M in Quincy Ill 25 Jul by Rev Kendall, William Connolly Jr. and Miss M. C. Greenley, both of this county.

Sara wife of Thomas J. Earickson d in Greensborough Sat (29 Jul), age about 40.

AU 24 Aug 1871/M 15 Aug at Concord Church by Rev J. B. Quigg Presiding Elder of Easton Dist during Camp, Rev W. J. Duhadaway of Wilmington Conference and Miss Harriett Corkran of this county.

The reunion of the surviving family of the late Short A. Willis of this county included three sons: A. J. Willis, P. J. Willis and R. S. Willis, the last two named res Galveston Texas; sister and a number of grandchildren some of them res in this county and others scattered over a wide distance of country from Massachussetts to Texas.

AU 7 Sep 1871/M 5 Sep by Rev John Erwin, James L. Pepper and Miss Mahala Parvis.

Newspaper Abstracts

AU 21 Sep 1871/John Collison of this county who has reached his 84th year informed us that he performed a journey on foot of 14 miles.

Mrs. Catharine Adams consort of the late Roger Adams d at the res of Anderton Liden 4 Aug, age 76 yrs, 6 mos and 5 das.

Galena infant d/o R. K. and Mary Collison d 9 Sep, age 3 mos and 13 das.

Edward Wilson d at his res near Greensborough 5 Aug age 82 yrs, 7 mos and 1 day. "He was one of the oldest and most respected citizen of the 2nd dist."

AU 28 Sep 1871/"An old colored woman known as 'Aunt Eve' years ago the slave of the late James Dukes died in Denton on Sunday night last (24 Sep) supposed to be about 90 years of age..."

M in Easton Thurs 14 Sep at St. Pauls M.E. Church by Rev George A. Phoebus, Thomas H. Covey and Miss Molly J. Roberts, all of Talb Co.

M in St. Joseph Mo 27 Aug by Rev M. M. Gawkins, Thomas J. Smith formerly of Denton to Miss M. Onie DeVinney of St. Josephs.

Mrs. Sinah Handy d 25 Sep at her res in the 4th dist, age 76. She was the wid of the late Trusten Handy and a member of the Baptist Church.

Joseph Pearson d at his res near Denton Wed morning 27 Sep after a lingering illness.

AU 5 Oct 1871/M at Whitins Station Mass by Rev J. W. Briggs, David Stone of Kansas City Mo to Dora Carleton Grey formerly of Caroline Co.

M Wed Sep 27th in Trinity M.E. Church East New Market by Rev N. M. Browne, Mr. R. O. Christian to Miss Fannie Charles, both of this county.

Francis Roe, age about 22, d 26 Sep near Denton of typhoid fever.

Dr. Walter Turpin, age 64, d at his res near Centreville Fri night 22 Sep after a protracted illness.

Mrs. G. Gamble, age 24, 3 mos and 4 das d at Federalsburg 20 Oct; she was the wife of Samuel B. Gamble.

AU 12 Oct 1871/Samuel W. Carpenter s/o Samuel J. and Sarah J. Carpenter d near Long Woods 3 Oct age 11 yrs.

AU 19 Oct 1871/M in St. Andrews Church Wilmington Del 3 Oct by Rt. Rev Bishop Lee, D. D., Henry Rollie of Denton to Miss Clara H. Adams of Del.

AU 26 Oct 1871/Jacob Chilcutt res near Bethlehem accidently cut himself with an axe 12 Oct and d from inflamation of the wound on the following Sun morning (15 Oct), age about 30.

M 17 Oct at Phila by Rev William R. McFarlane (brother of the bride), H. C. Friell, New York, to Mrs. Isabella R. Bearse of Hillsboro.

Millie d/o P. D. and Christina Hubbard d near Fowling Creek 11 Oct age 2 yrs and 6 mos.

Alex Whiteley, age 50, d at Upper Hunting Creek 16 Oct.

AU 2 Nov 1871/"Mr. Robert Thawley a prominent citizen resident near Hillsborough died at his residence Friday evening last (27 Oct)... He was born and raised in the second election district age about 66. (He was) a thrifty and prosperous farmer and had accumulated much of this world's goods, ... a good citizen, noble hearted, and generous..."

Newspaper Abstracts

Armilla Hubbard d/o Poulson E. and Christiana Hubbard d near Fowling Creek Wed morning 11 Oct, age 2 yrs, 6 mos and 26 das.

AU 23 Nov 1871/M Tues night (21 Nov) by Rev James H. Rich, Joshua L. Beachamp and Miss Eliza Roe, all of this county.

Mrs. Elizabeth Millington formerly of this place and wid of the late James T. Millington d in Milford 16 Nov, age 65.

AU 14 Jan 1875/Cecil Co: Charles H. Graham s/o C. C. Graham age 13 yrs was drowned in Northeast River between Charleston and Carpenter's Point while skating on the first of Jan.

QA Co: James W. Coleman an old and well known citizen of QA Co d at Crumpton 30 Dec age 77.

M at Smyrna Del 23 Dec 1874 by Rev G. A. Phoebus, Joshua M. Anthony and Miss M. Ella Lowe both of Caroline Co.

M 6 inst by Rev E. P. Aldred, Mr. G. P. Brittenham of Whitleysburg Del and Miss C. A. Moore of Caroline Co.

M 6 inst by Rev. E. P. Aldred, John Carroll and Miss Ida Williams both of this county.

M 21 Dec by Rev J. S. Willis, Luther Black and Sarah Wisher.

M 5th inst by Rev J. S. Willis, Joshua Bell and Nancy E. Fountain.

AU 21 Jan 1875/Kent: Capt Alex Wilson of Kent Co d last week.

Talb - Stephen Denny d at his res near Royal Oak last week over 90 yrs of age.

M near Friendship Thurs 7 Jan by Rev J. L. Kenney, Joshua Covey and Miss Amanda Smith all of this county.

M 6th inst by Rev J. S. Rich, James H. Harris to Miss ___ Keets both of this county.

M 12th inst at the M.E. Parsonage by T. S. Williams, Robert Russum and Miss Laura Willis all of this county.

M 13th inst at the res of Walter Massey by T. S. Williams, Robert E. Wilson of QA Co and Miss Kate N. Jump of Caroline Co.

M 14th inst by T. S. Williams, Eugene Dill and Miss Mary Nasby.

AU 21 Jan 1875/M 13 Jan at Chaple M.E. Church on Hillsborough circuit by Rev T. B. Killum, James Roe and Miss Clara Stoops all of this county.

M at Friendship M.E. Church Tues evening last by Rev J. U. Neill, Robinson Nichols and Miss Mary A. Nichols all of this county.

M Tues 8 Dec 1874 at the res of the bride's father by Rev Dr. Graybill, Rev H. C. Gearheart of the Balt Conference M.E. Church, south, to Miss Sophia V. Haas of Hardy Co West Va.

M 19 Jan at the res of the bride's father, Clement Noble,by Rev E. P. Aldred, Willis Liden and Miss Martha E. Noble, both of this county.

D at the res of his father in this county Sun last, Frank E. Williamson, age 24 yrs, 7 mos, 11 das.

D 18 inst near Andersontown, Mrs. Esther Poole consort of the late Henry Poole in the 83rd year of her age.

Newspaper Abstracts

D 16 Jan at the res of her husband, Levi Dukes, in Tuakahoe Neck, Mrs. Susan Dukes in the 76th yr of her age of pleurisey.

AU 4 Feb 1875/M 28 ult by Rev E. P. Aldred, Eli K. Smith and Miss Annie E. Anderson both of Caroline Co.

M Thurs 21st by Rev C. S. Terreyson, John Clark of QA Co to Miss Martha Spencer of Caroline Co.

M Joshua Chance of QA Co and Miss Annie Wyatt of Caroline Co 28th ult by Rev Vaughn Smith at the res of Thomas Wyatt.

M in Balt 28th ult by Rev Joseph B. Still, Rev Isaac G. Fosnotch of the Wilmington M.E. Conference and Bessie J. Burke of Balt.

M in Balt 19th inst by Rev Ward, Thomas Carmine of Caroline Co and Miss Mary F. Stevens of Balt.

M 2nd inst at Keene's Landing by Rev E. P. Aldred, Mr. C. Morgan Williams of Federalsburg and Miss Libbie Fulton of the former place.

AU 11 Feb 1875/Joseph Turner s/o Ferdinand Baynard age about 12 yrs who was so badly injured by the explosion of a gun in his hands several weeks ago since, died on Sat last at his fathers res near Burrsville Del.

Miss Cora F. Willis d/o Dr. H. F. Willis near Preston was found dead in her bed at the res of Dr. A. Hardcastle in the first election dist Thurs morning last ... age about 19 yrs...She was engaged as a teacher at Castle Hall School and boarded in the family of Dr. Hardcastle nearby.

D at his father's res in this county Fri last consumption, Draper A. Deweese s/o William H. Deweese, age 23 yrs.

D at his res near Federalsburg 28 Jan, Jackson O'Day age 63 yrs.

AU 18 Feb 1875/D at his res in Tuckahoe Neck Sat last, Levi Dukes age about 68 yrs.

D at his res in QA Co 13th inst Isaac Mason, age about 80 yrs.

D in the 1st election dist Mon last Sordan Kinnaman age about 80 yrs.

D at the Alms House in this county Thurs last Henry Cooper age about 80 yrs, formerly of Kent Co. He was a soldier in the war of 1812.

AU 25 Feb 1875/Jacob Alburger the postmaster at his place d at his res in this town Sun night last in the 59th year of his age... his disease was that of chronic dysentery...was a native of QA Co but removed to this county about 1834 and has res in this town ever since...postmaster at this place for the past 20 yrs except for 12 or 18 months during the administration of President Johnson... interred in the M.E. Churchyard... a member of the Masonic order.

M 11 inst in Balt City by Rev Jones, Thomas H. Slaughter of this county and Miss Georgia Taylor of Balt City.

D at Greensborough 20th inst Mrs. Mary Fowler wid of the late Clement Fowler aged about 85 yrs.

D at Greensborough Thurs morning last Mrs. Cannon wife of Hugh Cannon aged about 80 yrs.

AU 4 Mar 1875/D at Greensborough 14 Feb James Thomas s/o Jesse L. and Annie E. Turner, age 2 yrs and 3 mos.

-27-

M 2nd inst in Concord M.E. Church by Rev Aldred, H. Franklin Stevens and Miss Emma E. Scott both of Caroline Co.

AU 11 Mar 1875/D at the res of Benjamin Anthony near the Oakes on Sat last after a protracted illness, Mrs. Lucretia Gill wid of the late William Gill and d/o Joseph and Anna Anthony aged about 60 yrs.

D at Greensborough on Sat last after several weeks illness Rev Robert E. Kemp member of the Wilmington Annual Conference aged about 72 yrs.

AU 18 Mar 1875/D 13th inst at Hillsborough, James Morgan after a lingering illness age 24 yrs.

D near Preston 23rd ult of pneumonia Mrs. Ann Stafford wife of John O. Stafford in the 40th yr of her age.

D near Henderson 11th inst of scarlet fever, Mollie eldest d/o Eliza Jane and William M. Price, age 7 yrs, 9 mos, 6 das.

AU 18 Mar 1875/D 24 Dec 1874 at the res of his uncle, Alfred Davis, near Federalsburg, Jonathan Neal, youngest s/o Arthur and Sara A. Neal of Sussex Co Del, age 21 yrs, 6 mos, 7 das.

AU 25 Mar 1875/D Mon last, Bessie infant d/o Ella and Charles A. Dunning age about 7 weeks.

D near Ridgely Tues last of pneumonia Mrs. Thompson formerly of New York.

AU 1 Apr 1875/Jesse F. Butler s/o the late Jesse Butler of this county age about 19 yrs d very suddenly at the res of Mr. Morgan 2 1/2 miles from town on Mon evening last. He was assisting Mr. Morgan who was at work on a cart body near the dwelling when he staggered and fell back.

M 24th ult at the bride's father by Rev D. R. Wright, James L. Towers of Talb Co and Miss Sarah A. Payne of Caroline Co.

D at the res of his brother William M. Kirkman in Tuckahoe Neck on Tues last (31 Mar) after a lingering illness of consumption, Isaac W. Kirkman, age 30 yrs, 3 mos, 6 das.

AU 8 Apr 1875/D in Greensborough Mon last, Hughett Cannon, formerly of Del.

AU 15 Apr 1875/George W. Buck a citizen of the 1st dist res near Goldsborough was afflicted with paralysis on Mon last, the left side, arm and leg being useless and his articulation indistinct and unintelligible. No hopes are entertained of his recovery.

AU 22 Apr 1875/M 15th inst in Concord M.E. Church by Rev E. P. Aldred, Francis T. Willoughby and Miss Mary A. Coulbourn all of this county.

D 16th inst at the Brick Mills after a long and protracted illness, Mrs. Maria Smith in the 66th year of her age.

D at his res in this place Sat morning last, Owen C. Jones in 75th yr.

D at Milford Del on 14th inst of pulmonary consumption Harry Hemmons Councell s/o the late Samuel Councell of Greensborough, age 17 yrs.

D 10th inst West Troy, New York, Mrs. Emila J. Mason, formerly of this county, age 36 yrs, 1 mo, 7 das.

AU 29 Apr 1875/M near Hillsborough 22nd inst by Rev W. J. Duhadway, Baptist Smith and Miss Maggie Cahall both of this county.

Newspaper Abstracts

D 20th inst at the res of her uncle Mr. I. W. Jump in Talb Co, Miss Eva Green d/o the late Andrew S. Green of this county, age 19 yrs.

D at Greensborough Sun night last, William T. Warner late of Phila, age 33.

D at Greensborough Sun last, Mrs. Sarah Sangston wid of the late John A. Sangston, age 86.

D at her res near Cabin Creek Dorch Co Tues 19 Apr Mrs. Elenor Nichols wid of the late James Nichols, age 65.

AU 6 May 1875/M 29th ult at the Concord M.E. Church by Rev James H. Rich, John H. Todd and Miss Sarah E. Alford all of this county.

M 29th ult by Rev James H. Rich, Henry Francis Wilson and Miss Elenor Dixon all of this county.

AU 13 May 1875/The boiler attached to the steam saw owned by Mr. Patten in the neighborhood of Adamsville, Kent Co, Del exploded Sat afternoon last making a complete wreck of the boiler, killing the sawyer instantly and knocking two other men senseless for a short time ...The engineer had but a few minutes before left the engine when Mr. Bullock, the sawyer, stepped to the engine and was heard to remark that the water was too low in the boiler and it is supposed set the pump to work to supply the boiler with water. The cold water forced into a red hot boiler is supposed to have caused the explosion.

D Mon last near Bloomery Church Mrs. Sallie Murphy age about 60 yrs.

M on the evening of Apr 13th in Tuckahoe Neck by Rev Crouse, George W. Porter and Miss Charlotte A. Conner both of this county.

AU 20 May 1875/M 13th inst by Rev E. P. Aldred, Nathaniel Horsey and Miss Sallie C. Sangston, both of Greensborough.

D Wed last 28th ult near Marydel, John W. Downes, over 60 yrs of age.

D at his res in Frederica Del suddenly with apoplexy on the 8th inst, Capt James S. Downes, aged 79 yrs and 9 mos.

AU 27 May 1875/A colored woman res in the northern limits of the town named Hester Smith d very suddenly on Mon evening last.

Stanford Potter, a worthy colored man, for many years a citizen of this place and well known as a worthy mechanic, d at his res in this town Thurs morning last. Stanford was a blacksmith by trade. He was about 64 yrs old.

A private letter from Blooming Grove Indiana informs as of the death of William Norris on the 18th inst aged 71 yrs, 8 mos, 23 das, after a protracted illness of more than 6 mos. Mr. Norris was born in this county and continued to res here until Dec 1871. Previous to his removal west he res in this town. He leaves a wid and 10 children.

AU 27 May 1875/William M. Pearce scarcely in the prime of life d at his res near this place Tues evening last of pneumonia. This illness was but of a few days duration. He was a member of the first Eastern Shore Regiment. He leaves a wid and two small children. (A long item)

M at the Harmony M.E. Church Tues evening last by Rev J. O'Neill, E. Madison Towers and Miss Mollie D. Todd all of this county.

D 21 May at Leipsic Del, Mary Roe formerly of this county age 79 yrs.

Newspaper Abstracts

AU 3 Jun 1875/George W. Bryant, member of the bar from Harford Co, has removed to Denton and is practicing his profession in conjunction with his brother J. W. Bryant.

M at Preston 18 May by Rev D. R. Wright, Samuel R. Hopkins and Miss May Kinnamon, both of this county.

M 26 May by Rev D. R. Wright, William T. Cuyer of Talb Co and Miss Amelia J. Carroll of Caroline Co.

M 27th inst at the M.E. parsonage by Rev E. P. Aldred, Casper Schlittler and Miss Josephine Reed all of this county.

M at the M.E. Church in Denton on the 26th by Rev R. W. Todd assisted by Rev E. P. Aldred, Edward L. White of Easton and Miss Emma A. Harris of Caroline Co.

AU 10 Jun 1875/Mr. A. G. Gullet a former citizen of this town committed suicide in Phila on Thurs last by shooting himself in the region of the heart while laboring under a temporary fit of insanity... His remains were brought to this place Tues morning last and interred in the M.E. churchyard. Mr. Gullet was born in the lower part of Kent Co Del, came to reside in this place in 1844 being then about 17 yrs of age... In 1848 he became part owner of the Denton Journal ... was aged about 47 yrs.

M 26 May at the M.E. parsonage in Millington by Rev W. M. Warner, James S. Willis and Mrs. Annie M. Smith both of this county.

M 2nd inst at the res of the bride's father by Rev E. P. Aldred, Frederick Howard and Miss Sallie P. Andrew both of this county.

M on the 3rd inst at Concord M.E. Church by Rev E. P. Aldred, Alexander Nichols and Miss Sarah E. Murphy both of this county.

M at the home of the bride's parents 1 Jun by Rev E. H. Hynson, William C. Clark of Templeville Md and Miss Annie Smith of Kent Co Del.

M on the 3rd inst in Preston by Rev D. R. Wright, William Ross of Dorch and Miss Mary E. Perry of Caroline Co.

AU 17 Jun 1875/M 10th inst in Preston M.E. Church by Rev O'Neil, Thomas F. Cox and Miss L. Annie Harris all of this county.

M Wed 9 Jun at the res of the bride's parents by Rev Dr. L. F. Morgan, Mr. F. G. Dorsey and Miss Nellie R. d/o William S. Goslin all of Balt.

M at St. Mark's P.E. Church Wed 9 Jun by Rev Fleming James, William A. Thompson of Kent Island and Miss Florence V. Hungerford of Balt City.

D at his res in this county 10th inst after a lingering illness, Thomas Jones Sr in the 78th year of his age.

AU 24 Jun 1875/M 17 inst at Concord M.E. Church by Rev E. P. Aldred, Alexander Beachamp and Miss L. Breeding both of Caroline Co.

D at Federalsburg Wed 16th inst Lillian Smedley infant d/o W. H. and Hattie Alburger, age about 5 weeks.

AU 1 Jul 1875/D Sat 19 ult of consumption Mrs. Maggie Gootee wife of John Gootee.

D at the res of her husband near Hillsborough 21st ult, Levina E. Kemp after a lingering illness, age 32 yrs, 3 mos, 9 das.

Newspaper Abstracts

D 20 Jun at Henderson age 18 Cora F. Spencer d/o R. A. and Lucretia Spencer; interred on the 22nd in Silver Lake Cemetery, Dover Del.

M at the res of the bride's father Mon morning last by Rev Smithson, Rev James D. Reese of the Illinois Annual Conference of the M.E. Church, South, to Miss Emma D. Pippen d/o James Pippen of this county.

AU 8 Jul 1875/M in Phila 3 Jul by Rev J. T. Kenney at the res of Mr. F. Willis, Archibald McNair and Miss Sarah E. Fisher, both of Wyoming Del.

A young man name William Harper, s/o the late Allen Harper, was drowned in the pond at Smith's Mill in this county Wed 30 Jun. He went to Mr. Bullock's store nearby on that day which he left in company with a lad to the pond to bathe. He ventured out in deep water and being unable to swim was drowned.

AU 15 Jul 1875/M Sun night last by Rev Holmes, Thomas Garrett and Mrs. Lida Blackiston, both of this co.

M 7th inst in Preston by Rev D. R. Wright, William H. Bowdel and Miss Aramantha Wright oldest d/o Curtis A. Wright, all of this county.

M at the house of the bride's parents 1 Jul by Rev E. H. Hynson assisted by Rev James R. Dill, father of the bride, James S. Clark and Miss Emma S. Dill, both of Templeville.

AU 22 Jul 1875/D at Wilmington Del 2 Jul of cholera infantum, Willie, only s/o James D. and Mary Wilson formerly of this county, age 3 mos.

AU 5 Aug 1875/D in this town Sun night last of cholera infantum, Thomas Leonard, infant s/o Capt Thomas E. and Julia Heather, age 11 mos and 6 das.

AU 19 Aug 1875/M 17th inst at the M.E. Church, South, by Rev W. W. Watts, Bennett Downes of QA Co and Miss Kate Slaughter of Caroline Co.

D in Easton Wed 11th inst after a protracted illness, Mrs. Emma A., wife of Edward White, age 24 yrs, just married 11 weeks.

D in Wilmington 9th inst after an illness of 8 mos, Miss Willie S. d/o Edward Pritchett of this palce, age 14 yrs.

D at Federalsburg Mon last after an illness of 6 weeks, Mrs. Charlott Charles wife of W. H. Charles, age about 48 yrs.

D Fri last of brain fever, Thomas Potts, age about 32 yrs.

D Sun afternoon last in this town, Thomas Emory infant s/o Capt Thomas E. and Julia Heather, age 3 weeks and 3 das.

D at his res near Federalsburg 13th inst, Daniel Nichols, age 83 yrs.

AU 26 Aug 1875/Thomas DeRochbrune a former citizen of this county and at one time a member of the board of County Commissioners d at his res in QA Co Sun 15th inst in the 83rd year of his age.

A young man named Francis Melvin of this county, but for a short time past employed as head brakeman on the freight train No 3 on the Phila and Balt Railroad was killed a few hundred yards below the Delaware junction last week. He was riding on top of the cars and while passing under Moody's Bridge was struck on the head and killed instantly. The body was picked up and forwarded to a brother at Phila and was interred at Burrsville in this county Sun last.

D near Denton Fri morning last of heart disease, Walter, youngest s/o Capt R. R. Emerson, age 7 yrs, 6 mos and 3 das.

M Wed morning 18th inst at the res of the bride's mother by Rev William Warner, William R. Cahoon Jr and Miss Annie E. Burgess, both of Dover Del.

M 18th inst in M.E. Church Cambridge by Rev E. P. Aldred, Capt Elisha Calloway and Miss Lena Chaffinch, both of Potters Landing.

M at Harmony Wed 10th inst by Rev Lane, Robert H. Collison and Miss Martha Kimmey, all of this county.

M at Harrington Del 11th inst by Rev J. H. Mobry, Eli Massey and Mrs. Irena Smith, both of this county.

AU 2 Sep 1875/D in Federalsburg 29 Jul 1875 of Enteritis, Mollie A. wife of Joseph F. James and d/o Alfred and Mary Davis of Caroline Co, age 28 yrs, 6 mos and 14 das. She "leaves three interesting little ones."

D in Chestertown 25 Aug Tamsey Williams infant d/o E. T. and Mary N. Willis, age 1 yr, 1 mo and 27 das.

D 15 inst after a protracted illness of consumption at the res of Rev William Warner in Millington, Mrs. Kate Kene Anderson relict of John T. Anderson, age 29 yrs.

D at her father's res near Denton 24 Aug Miss Josephine Dukes, age 17 yrs.

D at Hillsborough 28 Aug Ruliff L. Duhadway only child of Rev W. J. and H. L. Duhadway, age 17 mos and 21 das.

AU 9 Sep 1875/Mrs. Burke wife of Rev G. W. Burke of the Wilmington Annual Conference d at the Delmar parsonage 26 Aug; she was the d/o the late John S. See and was born and raised at Hillsborough.

M Wed 1 Sep at Sheppard's M.E. Church by Rev Edward Davis assisted by Rev Holmes, Dr. Benial L. Lewis and Miss Georgia Sorden, both of this county.

D near Potters Landing 14 Jul Vaughn Omen infant s/o James H. and Mary E. Pool age 10 mos and 20 das.

AU 16 Sep 1875/A young woman named Amanda Deford committed suicide on Low Street Balt on Sat night last. She was about 24 yrs of age and is said to have been formerly of this county. She m a man by the name of W. Deford but they lived together only a few months. It is said her mother, Mrs. Martha E. Collison res near Greensborough. (A long item)

M 2nd inst at Thawleys Chapel by Rev W. J. Duhadaway, William Reynolds and Miss Caroline Hutchinson.

D at the res of her brother Henry Jarrell in Greensborough on the 17th inst, Miss Margarett Jarrell, age 20 yrs.

D near Burrsville Mon last, Mrs. Eliza A. Satterfield wife of John Satterfield age about 45 yrs.

D at Hillsborough Fri 3 Sep, Mary Seth infant child of Dr. T. S. and K. E. Holt, age about 2 mos.

D in Cambrigde 1st inst, Hennie K. d/o J. B. and Hennie Fletcher of Preston, age 14 mos.

D at his res near Vernon Del 13th inst, Eli Wroten age about 83 yrs.

AU 23 Sep 1875/M at the M.E. Church in this place Sat evening last by Rev E. P. Aldred, Col A. J. Willis and Miss Belle Rawlings, all of this county.

Newspaper Abstracts

AU 30 Sep 1875/D at Gilpin's Point Md, Cora Ellen infant d/o W. T. and Annie
E. Love, age 6 mos and 10 das.

Mrs. Mary E. Dawson consort of John Dawson d at her res at Skipton, Talb Co
16th inst in the 42 yr of her age.

D near Ridgely on the 20th inst, Sofa d/o Owen and Annie Lynch in the 6th yr.

D at the res of her father near Centreville, Nettie d/o Andrew J. and Louisa
Thawley, age 7 yrs, 11 mos, 9 das.

AU 7 Oct 1875/M 28th ult at the res of ex-sheriff Noble by Rev E. P. Aldred,
John W. Purt and Miss Hattie Noble, all of this county.

AU 14 Oct 1875/D at the res of James R. Manship near Concord in this county
Wed 6th inst Mrs. Elizabeth Peters in the 76th yr of her age.

AU 21 Oct 1875/D in Greensborough Sun morning last of typhoid fever, James M.
Warner, age about 28 yrs.

AU 28 Oct 1875/D 4 Aug near Bridgetown of cholera infantum, Kate Truefitt,
infant d/o Dr. L. W. Evans, age 10 mos.

AU 4 Nov 1875/M at St. Pauls M.E. Church 28th ult by Rev James H. Rich,
Eugene L. Sparklin and Miss Mary C. Hardesty, both of Talb Co.

AU 11 Nov 1875/D in this county Mon last, Perdue Keets, age 73 yrs.

M 4th inst in the M.E. Church of this town by Rev E. P. Aldred, William J.
Williamson and Miss Eliza J. Beachamp, all of this county.

AU 18 Nov 1875/Mrs. Hester Authors res near Marydel is said to be the oldest
person in that section of the county. She is 114 yrs old and was present
at Independence Hall at the signing of the Declaration of Independence.

M in Easton 3 Nov by Rev J. T. Lassell, John R. McQuay of Talb Co and Miss
Margaret A. Kennard of Caroline Co.

AU 25 Nov 1875/M in Church Hill 18 Nov George C. Tatman of Caroline and Miss
Annie B. Hurlock of QA Co.

M Sun evening last at the res of the bride's father near Denton by Rev James
H. Rich, Elisha F. Wilson and Miss Emily P. Anthony, all of this county.

M 18 Nov at the bride's father's by Rev D. R. Wright, David T. Perry and Mrs.
Mary T. Gootee all of this county.

AU 2 Dec 1875/M in the P.E. Church at Centreville QA Co Thurs last by the Rev
James A. Mitchell, William Spry Sherman and Miss L. Minnie Larrimore only d/o
T. F. Larrimore of QA Co.

M 30th ult at Concord M.E. Church by Rev E. P. Aldred, John Layton and Miss
Anna Breeding all of this county.

D at Greensborough Wed 25th inst Mrs. Ellen Horsey relict of the late Samuel
H. Horsey.

D in Easton 21st inst Sadie Estelle age 4 yrs, 2 mos, 20 das, only d/o of
Lewis and Sallie R. Flynn.

D at his res in this county 29 Nov, William Boyce age about 60 yrs.

AU 9 Dec 1875/M 1st inst at the M.E. parsonage Denton by Rev E. P. Aldred,
Thomas F. Roe and Miss Ellen Dukes, all of this county.

M 2nd inst at the M.E. Parsonage Denton by Rev E. P. Aldred, Albert Satterfield and Miss Eunity E. Roe, all of this county.

M Thurs 25th ult by Rev G. F. Beaven, T. Bascom Saulsbury of Talb Co and Miss Mollie H. Bonwell of QA Co.

D at his res near Greensborough Sat morning last, William Hollingsworth after a lingering illness.

AU 16 Dec 1875/On Sun last Samuel Butler an old colored man about 70 yrs old was jailed for shooting his own son on Sat night last. He res near Preston in the 4th dist. Their quarrel originated about a horse his son, Kelly Butler, had rode off. In the struggle a gun was discharged. He d next day, age 23.

M in the evening of 24 Nov at the res of the bride's parents in New York City by Rev B. F. Price, James M. Price s/o the officiating minister to Miss Lizzie Potter.

M on the 9th inst by Rev E. P. Aldred, Elias T. Elliott of Millsboro Del and Miss Mary R. Wagaman of Caroline Co.

M in Seaford Del 2 Dec by Rev W. H. Hutchins, Thomas H. Duling of Talb Co to Miss Mary E. Lord of Seaford Del.

M in Bridgeville Del Tues evening 2 Dec by Rev W. H. Hutchins, Joseph N. Johns, M. D., of Seaford to Miss Hattie Layton of Bridgeville.

M the 13th inst at the M.E. Parsonage Denton by Rev E. P. Aldred, Mr. W. A. Warner and Miss Lizzie E. Latshaw, all of this county.

M at the M.E. Church Denton on the 15th by Rev E. P. Aldred, William T. Wilson of Milford Del and Miss Sallie C. Morgan of this county.

AU 23 Dec 1875/D Fri last near Marshy Hope Bridge, Sussex Co Del, Levin Todd age 80 yrs.

M at the M.E. Parsonage Federalsburg on the 15th inst by Rev William J. O'Neill, James T. Bowdell and Miss Nelly Pritchett, all of this county.

M 21st inst at the res of the Bride's father by Rev E. P. Aldred, Fred W. Towns and Miss Roxie Stevens, all of this county.

DJ 18 Nov 1876/M in Phila 23 Oct by Rev James Mathews, Samuel J. Tolson, formerly of this county and Miss Mollie D. Faries of Smyrna Del.

M 7 Nov by Rev J. L. Straughn, Robert J. Rawley of Del to Miss Alice Carter of Caroline Co.

D near American Corner Caroline Co Thurs 2 Nov, Robert Warner, formerly of Talb Co, over 80 yrs of age.

D at his father's res near Burrsville Fri last William Webber s/o William Webber, age about 19 yrs and 1 mo.

D 10th inst at his res in thic county, Thomas A. Sorden; he was born 2 Sep 1847. (A long item.)

D 25 Nov Capt Alexander Stewart, one of the oldest and most estimable citizens of our town on Sun last 19th inst, of consumption, age 60 yrs.

DJ 25 Nov 1876/M 23rd inst at M.E. Parsonage in Denton, by Rev E. P. Aldred, John F. Sullivan and Mrs. Dorcus Andrew, all of this county.

M on the 19th inst in Denton by Rev E. P. Aldred, Theodore R. Berry and Miss Elizabeth M. Fitsgerald, all of this county.

Newspaper Abstracts

D at his res near Denton Sat morning last of pneumonia, William Sorden, age 70 yrs.

DJ 2 Dec 1876/M 15th ult at the Preston M. E. Church by Rev T. J. Prettyman of Wicomico Co, Columbus Waddell and Miss Belle Trice.

M near Marydel 19 Nov by Rev E. H. Hynson, Nathaniel Smith of this county and Miss Mary J. Poor of Kent Co Del.

M at Marydel by Rev E. H. Hynson, George T. Johnson and Miss Susan Barcus, both of Kent Co Del.

M at the res of John T. Wilson, 601 Jefferson St. Wilmington Del, by Rev J. E. Smith, Beniah L. Fleming of Easton and Miss Emma Jarman of this county.

M 28th ult by Rev E. P. Aldred at the M.E. Parsonage Denton, H. Clay Chaffinch and Miss Emma E. Holbrook, all of this county.

M 22 Nov by Rev J. L. Straughn, William T. Hayman and Miss Emma Draper, both of Kent Co Del.

D in Greensborough Sat last, Miss Sallie Insley age 19 yrs.

D in Balt City 24th ult, Miss Anna Hall formerly of this town, age about 24.

DJ 9 Dec 1876/M in the Abington Church Harf Co Md by Rev A. D. Melvin and W. M. Strayer officiating, Rev A. T. Melvin of Crumpton Md and Miss F. Marion Swartz of Harf Co.

M at the Presbyterian Church Federalsburg Thurs evening 30 Nov by Rev E. L. Boing, James O. Redhead of Federalsburg and Miss Winona Hutchinson, all of this county.

DJ 16 Dec 1876/M 12th inst by Rev W. J. Duhadaway, John K. Skinner of QA Co and Miss Annie M. Fleetwood of this county.

M at the res of the bride's parents on the 6th inst by Rev Treadway of the M.P. Church, Joseph Douglass and Miss Hellen Fields, eldest d/o Hon. Daniel Fields, all of this county.

M Balt City on 15th inst William A. Holbrook and Miss Maranda E. Calloway, both of this county.

M at Marydel 5th inst by Rev E. H. Hynson, Samuel H. Hudson and Miss Lucy B. Reed, all of this county.

M near Slaughters Station on the 17th inst by Rev E. H. Hynson, Joseph Walls of QA Co and Miss Mary L. Booker of Kent Co Del.

M 6th inst at St. Pauls Church Hillsboro by Rev George F. Beaven, George T. Hobb of QA Co and Miss Ada C. Gearhart of Caroline Co.

D at Marydel on the 10th inst, Miss Laura V. Walters age 19 yrs and 11 mos.

DJ 23 Dec 1876/M near Harmony 13 Dec by Rev D. R. Wright, William H. Collins of Talb Co and Miss Hester A. Story of Caroline Co.

M in Madison Avenue M.E. Church Balt 14 Dec by Rev J. T. Kenny assisted by Pastor Rev D. Stevenson, Mr. E. J. Kenny of Phila and Miss L. Virginia youngest d/o William Corkran of Balt City.

M at Hollisterville Pa by Rev O. C. Payne president of the Pennsylvania Annual Conference M.P. Church, William C. Willoughby of this county and Miss Estelle M. Payne d/o the officiating clergyman.

DJ 30 Dec 1876/M at the res of the bride's father in Caroline Co 20 Dec by Rev Rumsey Smithson, Capt Robert D. Todd of Talb Co and Miss Amanda D. Andrew.

M 6th inst at the M.E. Church Queenstown Md by Rev E. H. Miller, William C. McConner and Miss Florie E. Bryan, both of QA Co.

DJ 30 Dec 1876/M 20th inst at the M.E. Church Queenstown by Rev E. H. Miller, John D. Long to Mrs. Mary W. Seward, both of this county.

M 20 Dec at Shephards M.E. Church by Rev J. L. Straughn, Thomas P. Green of Kent Co Del and Miss Annie E. Lowe of Caroline Co.

M 28 inst James H. Nichols and Miss Millie Payne, all of this county.

M 26th inst in Concord M.E. Church by Rev E. P. Aldred, Edward W. Liden and Miss Ella Chaffinch, all of this county.

M 27th inst in the Congregational Church Potters Landing by Rev E. P. Aldred, Thomas L. Chaffinch and Miss Alexine J. Chaffinch, all of this county.

M at Hillsboro 27 Dec by Rev W. J. Duhadaway, Willis Andrew and Miss Mary Chance, both of QA Co.

D in this town Mon 25 Dec after an illness of a few days, Mrs. Elizabeth G. P. Steele, wife of James B. Steele in the 51st year of her age.

AU 4 Jan 1877/D at his res near Harris' Chapel in this county, 25th ult, John L. Bloxon, age about 57 yrs.

M 28th ult by Rev James E. Webb, James L. Thomas of Federalsburgh and Francis Collins of Oak Grove Del.

AU 11 Jan 1877/M at Marydel 19 Dec by Rev E. H. Hynson, Titus I. Pippin of Caroline Co and Miss Emma E. Colescott of Kent Co Del.

M 27 Dec near Bethlehem by Rev D. R. Wright, William H. Towers and Miss Polean Burkett, all of this county.

D at the res of his son-in-law,William T. Fleetwood in Tuckahoe Neck on Tues last after a short illness, Trustin P. Cannon formerly of Sussex Co Del, age 79 yrs, 9 mos, 26 das. Interment will take place at Harris' Chapel this day at 2 o'clock P.M.

D Mon morning last Ormand s/o J. T. Hutchins age about 13 yrs from the disease of pneumonia supervening upon rubeola.

DJ 13 Jan 1877/D 15 Dec Herman J. Layton age 9 mos and 8 das.

D 4th inst Annie M. wife of John Layton, age 24 yrs, 4 mos, 26 das.

M at Marydel 13 Dec by Rev E. H. Hynson, John T. Griffith and Miss Susanna Downs, both of Kent Co Del.

M near Henderson 21 Dec by Rev E. H. Hynson, Charles T. Betton of Centreville and Mrs. Mariam E. Godwin of Henderson of this county.

M at the res of Mr. J. H. Douglass of Preston 9 Jan by Rev J. E. Nicholson, John O. Stafford to Mrs. Lotta Daugherty, all of Caroline Co.

M 9th inst at M.E. Parsonage Denton by Rev E. P. Aldred, Robert G. Pepper and Miss Eliza A. Satterfield, all of this county.

M 10th inst at the M.E. Parsonage by Rev E. P. Aldred, Mr. A. T. Porter and Miss Hannah Pepper, all of this county.

M 10th inst at the res of the bride's father by Rev E. P. Aldred, Mr. T. Luther Framton and Miss Annah K. Nichols, all of this county.

M Thurs 11th inst at St. Peters Roman Catholic Church QA Co by Rev Henchy, William R. Griffith and Miss Lucy B. Richardson, both of this county.

AU 18 Jan 1877/Richard M. Legg res QA Co about 3 miles from Hillsborough d very suddenly Thurs last.

DJ 20 Jan 1877/M at St. Peters Church Queenstown 9th inst by Rev Father Hency, Mr. D. F. Rhodes and Miss Rettie A. Smith d/o S. N. Smith.

AU 25 Jan 1877/M 17 inst at Christ Church Denton by Rev E. J. Stearns, D. D., Rector, Dr. Frederick Straughn and Mrs. Corine Gullet d/o the late John R. T. Salisbury.

M 17th inst in Preston by Rev D. R. Wright, John Smith and Miss Mary V. Freizure, both of this county.

M 9th inst by Rev J. T. Van Burkalow, Mr. J. Melson and Miss Sallie Wright, eldestd/o Isaac K. Wright, all of Sussex Co Del.

M in Phila 10th inst by Rev Williams of Seaford Del, Asbury Brown and Miss Sallie S. Willis only d/o the late John S. Willis, all of Seaford Del.

AU 1 Feb 1877/Master Ernest, little s/o Rev E. P. Aldred held a birthday party.

M 24th inst at the res of the bride's father, Mr. J. W. Thawley by Rev E. P. Aldred, Mr. R. C. Garrett of Phila and Miss Laura B. Thawley of this county.

M 24th inst at the res of the bride's father in Denton by Rev E. P. Aldred, Mr. E. Todd and Mrs. M. M. Hynson d/o Thomas Melvin.

M near Whiteleysburg 11 Jan by Rev N. Genn, Hugh A. Haddaway and Miss Sarah M. Kirby, both of this county.

M 10th inst at the M.E. Church, South, Trappe, by Rev J. E. Reed, John Jarrell and Mrs. Lutie Wamsley of Talb Co.

M 18 Jan in the M. E. Church at Harrington by Rev W. F. Talbot, George A. Redden and Miss Francis A. Anderson, all of Kent Co Del.

D in Talb Co 3 Jan John Shaw formerly of this county age 73 yrs, 2 mos, 21 das.

D at the res of his father in Tuckahoe Neck in this county Sun morning last after a lingering illness, John W. Jewell s/o Luther W. Jewell, age 30 yrs, 4 mos, 29 das.

DJ 3 Feb 1877/M 23 Jan at the M. E. Church Marydel by Rev E. H. Hynson, John Bush and Miss Ella Ayers, both of Henderson, Caroline Co.

AU 8 Feb 1877/M 24th ult by Rev E. H. Hynson, George D. Walls and Miss M. A. Perkins, both of QA Co.

M in Hillsboro 31st ult by Rev J. W. Duhadaway, George Smith and Miss Ida E. Seward.

M on the 10th ult in the M. P. Church Burrsville by Rev John Lee Straughn, John E. Starkey and Miss E. E. Murphy, both of this county.

M 24th ult at the res of the bride's brother near Wye Mills by Rev T. J. Slaughter, Edmund L. Adams of Caroline Co and Miss Julia E. Harris of Talb Co.

D at her home in Greensborough 17th ult, Mrs. Sarah Elizabeth Ratliff in the 38th yr of pulmonary consumption, an invalid for many months. Her husband and two children survive her.

M 17 Jan by Rev E. H. Hynson, Alphonza Purnell of QA Co and Miss Huldah F. Nicherson of Kent Co Del.

AU 15 Feb 1877/M 7th inst at the M.E. Parsonage Denton by Rev E. P. Aldred, Henry M. Cade and Miss Georgia E. Park, all of this county.

M 8th inst at the M.E. Parsonage by Rev E. P. Aldred, Samuel Harrington and Miss Annie E. Langrell, all of this county.

M 13th inst at the res of the bride's father by Rev E. P. Aldred, James Hicks and Miss Annie Fleetwood, all of this county.

AU 22 Feb 1877/D at Marydel 15 Feb Anna wife of James Edward Stafford age 29 yrs and 6 mos.

AU 1 Mar 1877/Dr. William H. Dawson d very suddenly of heart disease Sun week while returning in his carriage from Broad Creek Neck to St. Michaels where he had been to visit a patient.

AU 8 Mar 1877/Mrs. Maria Stanton wid of the late James M. Stanton well known to many of our oldest citizens and a former citizen of this county d at the res of her son-in-law Peter Morris Lindale near Dover Sat the 25th; buried at Dover on Tues the 27th.

D in this town Fri last after a short illness, George Messick age 42 yrs.

DJ 10 Mar 1877/D near Bethlehem 20 Feb Mrs. Sarah Dillen wife of John A. Dillen in the 64th year.

AU 15 Mar 1877/M 28 Feb at M.E. Parsonage Dover Del by Rev J. H. Caldwell, James Lane and Miss Katie Moore of Kent Co Del.

D near Union Corner Sat the 3rd inst of consumption, Mrs. Emily Jewell wife of William K. Jewell age about 33 yrs.

D Thurs 8th inst at this res near Burrsville of asthma, William R. Jewell, age 41 yrs and 7 mos.

D at the res of Mrs. Serena Simpson near Greensborough 27 Feb after a protracted illness of consumption, Samuel Turner age about 36 yrs.

AU 22 Mar 1877/Rev E. P. Aldred who has for the past 3 yrs labored with great zeal and energy in our midst left on Tues last for Cecilton, Cecil Co.

M 15th inst at the res of the bride's father near Preston by Rev R. D. Bradley, Rev George T. Hardesty of the Wilmington Conference and Miss Annie M. Towers, all of this county.

M 15th inst by Rev James H. Rich, Charles M. Webber and Miss Nicy Wright, all of this county.

D near Union Grove in Caroline Co 12 Mar, Wesley Edwin s/o P. W. and M. E. Butler age 7 yrs.

D 16 Mar at Marydel in Caroline Co, Mrs. Mary Greenwell age 76 yrs.

AU 29 Mar 1877/M at the res of the bride's mother in Easton 20 Mar by Rev R. Smithson, Solomon Covey and Miss Mary E. Bowdle, both of Easton.

D of consumption 26 Mar at the res of Joseph T. Ewing in Trappe dist, Talb Co, Joseph T. Councell in the 33rd year. His remains were interred at Catholic Churchyard in this place Tues last.

D suddenly near Houston Branch, Caroline Co, Sat morning 17th inst, Elisha Eaton age 59.

DJ 31 Mar 1877/D 17 Feb near Greensborough Elinor D. Moore in the 73rd yr.

AU 5 Apr 1877/M 3rd inst at the res of the bride's sister by Rev J. Erwin, Elijah Luff of Wilmington Del and Miss Carrie Mitchell of Caroline Co.

D 27th ult in Phila Dr. William A. Tatem of St. George's Del in the 77th yr.

D at the res of her son-in-law Charles H. Rathel on the 28th ult Mrs. Lucretia Lister wife of James Lister in the 77th yr.

D in Talb Co in Feb last, Senah B. Willis formerly of Caroline Co and brother to Zaceria Willis, age about 75.

DJ 7 Apr 1877/D at the res of her daughter 24th ult, Eleanor Vinson relict of the late James Vinson, in the 72nd yr.

AU 12 Apr 1877/D near Federalsburg 4th inst, Bushrod Collins.

D near Federalsburg 31 Mar, of bronchitis, David W. Chipp, native of the Isle of Wight, England, in the 43rd year of his age.

D at Farmington Del 30 Mar, Herbert Powell, age 17 yrs.

D near Andersontown Fri morning last after a lingering illness, James W. Hignutt s/o Peter W. and Martha J. Hignutt age 13 yrs, 1 mo, 16 das.

D Tues last near Burrsville, Mrs. Duesse wife of William H. Duesse age about 45 yrs.

AU 19 Apr 1877/"The marriage license fee in Delaware has been reduced from $4.00 to $2.00. No more leaving the state now to get hitched up in double harness."

M 12th inst at Boonsboro, Caroline Co, by Rev N. McQuay assisted by Rev Albert Chandler, William H. Lewis of QA Co to Miss Ida Wyatt of Caroline Co.

M at Preston 12th inst by Rev D. R. Wright, William E. Adams and Miss Harriet A. Camper, all of this county.

M 31 Mar by Rev M. R. Watkinson, Samuel Fountain formerly of this county and Miss Mary E. Robertson of Balt City.

D in Bethlehem 12th inst George eldest s/o William H. and Margaret Blades in the 19th yr of his age.

D at Marydel 10th inst Mrs. Mary Elizabeth Bailey wife of John Bailey and d/o ex-Governor Polk, age 62 yrs and 10 mos.

AU 26 Apr 1877/Jesse Hubbard of Hunting Creek in the 4th dist is fitting up a cemetery on his land between Hunting Creek and Preston. (Long item)

M at Greensborough Tues 17th inst in the church of the Holy Trinity by Rev G. F. Beaven, Rector, Dr. Oscar Stansbury of Chicago, Calif, to Miss Libbie d/o J. P. Manlove.

M at Greensborough 5th inst in the church of the Holy Trinity by Rev G. F. Beaven, Rector, Dr. William Caulk of Talb Co to Miss Florence A. Turner.

M near Marydel 16 Apr by Rev E. H. Hynson, Joshua Sparks and Celia Harwood, both of Del.

D near Marydel 15 Apr Hester wife of Isaac Thomas age 44 yrs, 5 mos, 23 das.

AU 3 May 1877/M 24 Apr in Phila by Rev E. P. Aldred, William T. Vandyke of Cecilton and Miss Rosa Pratt of Sassafras, Kent Co Md.

Newspaper Abstracts

M 24th inst at the house of the bride's parents by Rev Charles Hill, Rev F.
C. McSorley of the Wilmington Conference to Miss A. Tryphena Roe d/o of James
Roe of Talb Co.

D at his res near Whiteleysburg Sun morning last after a brief illness Byard
Davis age 73 yrs.

AU 10 May 1877/M at Hillsboro Wed evening 9 May by Rev McQuay, William
Thawley and Miss Alice Flemming, both of this county.

D near Preston 2 May Isaac Fluharty age 86 yrs, 11 mos, 2 das.

D near Federalsburg 2nd inst Miss Fannie Stevenson wife of Thomas Stevenson
in the 58th year of her age.

AU 17 1877/The formal opening of Fairmount Cemetery situated on the lands of
Jesse Hubbard will take place Sun 27 May at 2 P.M.

DJ 19 May 1877/M 16th inst by Rev J. H. Kenney Col R. J. W. Garey and Miss
Vashti Saulsbury.

AU 31 May 1877/Barney Cannon s/o John M. Cannon at Bridgetown in this county
was one of the victims of the unfortunate launch of the iron steamship at
Chester Pa last week.

M Wed 10th inst by Rev George F. Beaven in St. Paul'e Chapel in Hillsboro,
John Symons and Mrs. S. E. Lomax, both of Talb Co.

M Thurs last 17th inst by Rev George F. Beaven in St. Paul's Chapel in
Hillsboro, Mr. I. Thomas Brown to Miss H. F. Eaton, both of this county.

M 24 May by Rev J. E. Nicholson at the res of the bride's father, William H.
Valliant and Miss Joanna Smoot, all of this county.

AU 7 Jun 1877/M at Bethlehem Church Taylors Island Dorch Co Thurs 24 May Dr.
Jacob L. Noble of Preston and Miss Mary E. Travers d/o Judge Levi D. Travers
of Taylors Island.

D near Greensboro 26th inst of pneumonia, William H. s/o William and
Henrietta Dyer age 20 yrs, 11 mos, 26 das.

D Sun morning 27 May at Dover, Mrs. Mary Nandian Cowgill Sr.

D at her res in Frederica Del 30 May Mrs. Catharine Hutson age 72 yrs.

AU 16 Jun 1877/D 10th inst Mrs. Jewell wife of Rev J. Jewell age 24 yrs and
8 mos.

AU 21 Jun 1877/Eddie Walker age about 13 yrs whose parents res in Phila was on
a visit among his friends when drowned in Liden's Mill Pond Fri afternoon
last. His remains were interred at the family burial grounds near Bridgeville
Del Sun afternoon last.

M near Felton Tues 12 Jun inst by Rev John Downham, James Philips and Miss
Lydia Wyatt, all of Kent Co Del.

M 13th inst by Rev T. S. Williams, G. Emmet Bell to Miss Mary B. Cartee, all
of Kent Co Del.

AU 5 Jul 1877/George Sparks s/o the wid of Solomon Sparks age about 8 yrs was
killed by lightning near Fairlee Kent Co.

M Sun 24th inst at the res of James Short by Rev J. R. Dill, Isaac W. Short
and Miss Veney Taylor, all of Kent Co Del.

Newspaper Abstracts

D at Urieville Kent Co Md Fri morning 29 Jun, Mollie R. d/o N. P. and Sallie R. Sewell age exactly 6 yrs.

DJ 7 Jul 1877/M Thurs evening 1 Mar by Rev Smith, R. M. Calpha to Mrs. Rhoda J. Martin, both of Brookville, Franklin Co, Indiana.

M at this town in the M.E. parsonage 3rd inst by Rev J. E. Smith, John W. Morgan of Caroline Co and Miss Laura J. Breeding of Kent Co Del.

AU 12 Jul 1877/Fannie Banks a colored woman with an infant in her arms was knocked over board by the jibing of the boom of a small sloop on the Nanticocke River Sun 1st inst. The infant was saved but the mother was drowned.

DJ 14 Jul 1877/M near Marydel 5 Jul by Rev E. H. Hynson, John C. Pippin and Miss Mollie Urry, both of this co.

M at the M.E. parsonage Federalsburg 3rd inst by Rev L. Jewell, Jacob T. Mobray and Sarah A. Hurlock.

AU 19 Jul 1877/Rev J. M. McCarter formerly of this county delivered an elequent oration on 4 Jul at Onancock Va.

M at Milton Del 4 Jul by Rev N. M. Brown, Presiding Elder of Salisbury dist assisted by Rev R. W. Todd, Rev William Wells Wolf Wilson pastor M.E. Church Salisbury to G. Anna Lank of Milton.

M Tues 10 Jul at Christ Church Easton by Rev Robert Wilson, William P. Powell and Evelyn Mary 2nd d/o Julius A. Johnson editor of the Eastern Ledger.

D near Federalsburg 8 Jul Mrs. Margaret Andrew relict of the late Melvin Andrew age 75.

D near Potters Landing 15 Jul Sun morning last Mrs. N. Elizabeth Hignutt wife of Dr. J. W. Hignutt, interred at Concord Church Mon last. (Also in DJ 28 Jul 1877)

AU 26 Jul 1877/Some thief entered Meadford's Mill on Sat night last and made off with a bag of flour.

D near Burrsville of paralysis Sun morning last Mrs. Harris wid of the late James Harris age about 60 yrs.

D at Easton Sun 22nd inst Mary Kersey infant d/o Eli H. and Mary E. F. Furniss age 9 mos and 13 das.

D near Denton Sat morning last James Howard infant s/o James T. and Sarah A. Sylvester age 3 mos and 7 das.

D at the res of his father Henry S. Fisher near Hillsborough 25th inst, Frederick Fisher age about 20 yrs.

DJ 4 Aug 1877/D in Preston 30th ult Agatha Hoskins d/o Dr. J. R. and Mrs. Sallie Phillips age 1 yr and 9 mos.

DJ 11 Aug 1877/D at Arrodondo Fla Mon 30th ult of congestion of the brain, Robert H. Wilson a native of Caroline Co age 45 yrs.

AU 16 Aug 1877/D near Preston 12th inst of typho-malarial fever, Miss Hester A., eldest d/o Henry W. and Elsie Northrop in the 36th yr.

D 29 Jul near Henderson, John C. s/o John W. Christopher age 30 yrs, 5 mos, 27 das.

Newspaper Abstracts

D in this town 4th inst Annie Estell infant d/o P. W. and Annie H. Downes, age 1 yr, 9 mos, 6 das.

D at the res of her husband E. Frank Wilson 3 Aug Emma d/o Thomas Butler in the 27th yr.

AU 23 Aug 1877/D near Greensboro 16 Aug Jennie d/o Jacob Stokely age about 4 yrs.

D 9th inst Minnie Cottingham youngest child of William H. and Elizabeth Lecompte age 1 yr and 6 mos.

AU 30 Aug 1877/D Mrs. Mary Stafford wife of James Stafford; she leaves a husband and child.

D near Hambleton 15th inst, Catharine A. Sparklin wife of Capt Samuel Sparklin in the 56th yr.

D at his res in the 4th dist in this county Tues last after a short illness, Mitchell Covey age about 63 yrs.

AU 6 Sep 1877/M by Rev J. A. Brindle at the bride's father near Greensboro, Joseph M. Rodph of Crumpton Kent Co Md to Miss Sarah F. Jackson.

AU 20 Sep 1877/M Thurs last by Rev Charles Ash, Obe Lewis and Wilmina Brown.

D 3rd inst in Denton, Sarah Jane infant d/o J. W. and Mary Jane Thompson, age 4 mos.

D at Federalsburg at the res of her brother-in-law, James O. Redhead on the 11th inst, Miss Lydia Hutchinson d/o Manlius P. Hutchinson age 19 yrs, 5 mos, 3 das.

AU 27 Sep 1877/"Mr. Seth H. Evitts an old and respected citizen of this county died at his residence near Andersontown on Saturday last, aged about 82 years. Mr. Evitts was born on the farm where he died and has resided there during his whole life. He has at various times filled the office of Justice of the Peace, was a very quiet citizen - was never married and up to within a few years past enjoyed good health. He had three sisters, neither of whom were ever married, each of which lived to over eighty years the last surviving sister dying a few years ago. He had two brothers each of whom 30 years ago conducted the mercantile business in this town. They also were well advanced in years."

D near Union Grove 11th inst Mrs. Beachamp w/o Levin Beachamp of heart disease age about 72 yrs.

AU 4 Oct 1877/D near Federalsburg 1 Oct Mrs. Martha B. Covey wid of the late Michell Covey in the 56th yr.

DJ 27 Oct 1877/D in Easton Tues 2 Oct, Mrs. Rebecca H. Newman in the 64th yr.

M Thurs 18 Oct at Hall X-road M.E. Church by Rev N. McQuay, Thomas Mulliken and Miss Susie Smith, both of QA Co.

AU 1 Nov 1877/A little child between two and three d/o Mr. and Mrs. John H. Bowdle in Del about two miles from Marydel was burned 23rd inst by her clothes taking fire at the stove hearth and d on the 25th.

AU 8 Nov 1877/Jonathan Bedwell d very suddenly while alone in his house in Marydel 2nd inst age 64 yrs.

AU 15 Nov 1877/M at the res of the bride's father near Preston 31 Oct by Rev

Newspaper Abstracts

D. R. Wright, Francis L. Perry and Miss Mary E. Connelly, both of this county.

M 30 Oct at the res of the bride's parents by Rev Charles Hill assisted by Rev T. L. Tómkinson, Rev E. H. Hoffecker of the Wilmington Conference to Miss Annie M. Stewart d/o Samuel Stewart of Talb Co.

M at the home of William Cranor by Rev N. Y. Genn, Alfred Raughly of Kent Co Del and Miss Mattie J. Wix of Greensborough.

AU 22 Nov 1877/D at Henderson on 19th inst of consumption, Charles youngest s/o William Hynson age 22 yrs and 20 das.

AU 29 Nov 1877/M at the res of Mr. Nichols near Concord 21st by Rev J. E. Smith, George Collins and Miss Sarah E. Trice, all of this county.

M at the res of Mrs. Adams in Tuckahoe Neck Tues the 27th inst by Rev J. E. Smith, Cornelius D. Bennett of Balt and Miss Rhoda A. Adams of this county.

AU 6 Dec 1877/M at the 2nd inst by Rev J. L. Kenny, Benny F. Payne Dorch Co and Miss Mollie J. Andrew of Caroline Co.

M on the 22nd ult by Rev J. L. Kenny, James A. Nichols and Miss Mary J. Frampton, all of this county.

M on the 21st ult at St. Peters Roman Catholic Church by Rev Father Henchy, James H. Colbourn and Miss Annie M. Evitts, both of this county.

D in Phila on the 12th ult of congestion of the brain, Isabella wife of F. E. H. Shields formerly of this county age about 41 yrs.

AU 13 Dec 1877/M at Still Pond 5th ult by Rev E. B. Newman, Charles A. Fountain to Miss Ida G. Carrow, all of Kent Co Md.

D at his res in Easton morning of the 10th inst Thomas Edgar in the 75th yr.

D in Hillsborough after a short illness Charles Beaven oldest child of James M. and Laura J. Wooters age 8 yrs, 10 mos, 15 das.

DJ 15 Dec 1877/M at the M.E. Church in Smyrna Del 5th inst by Rev E. Stubbs, George T. Baynard of Easton and Miss Bell Wilson of Smyrna.

DJ 22 Dec 1877/M 29 Nov last by Rev J. L. Kenny, William Allan and Miss Margaret A. Porter, all of this county.

M 13th inst at the res of William T. Lockerman by Rev J. E. Smith, Mr. C. C. Wright and Miss Margarette E. Robinson, all of Caroline Co.

M 13th inst at the res of the bride's father, Mr. T. S. Noble by Rev R. D. Bradley, Robert Jarrell and Miss Addie Noble.

M 17th inst on board the steamer R. D. Bradley by Rev R. D. Bradley, Francis M. Dean and Miss Sarah A. Dunham.

M at the res of the bride's moather in Preston 19 Dec, Dr. Jenkins of Federalsburg and Miss Lizzie Cox by Rev J. L. Kenny. The couple went to Balt on their bridal tour.

D near Federalsburg 8th inst William Butler age 87 yrs.

"Died at Potters Landing on the 17th inst at the residence of A. J. Willis of heart disease Miss Alice G. Jones aged 17 years. She had been attending school in Canada for the past three years; her health failing she returned home. She had just entered her 18th year ..."

Newspaper Abstracts

D after a brief illness, Ninian Pinkney, M.D., L.L.D., Medical Director, USN, native of Md, born 7 Jun 1811, d at his res in Londonderry near Easton 15 Dec.

DJ 29 Dec 1877/M near Slaughters' Del 19 Dec by Rev E. H. Hynson, John G. Reed and Miss Harriett B. Luff, both of Kent Co.

M near Henderson 20 Dec by Rev E. H. Hynson, James D. Jones and Miss Marianna Vincent, both of Caroline Co.

M at the M.E. Parsonage on the evening of the 27th by Rev J. E. Smith, Isaac Fleetwood and Miss Aramenta Robinson, all of this county.

D at his res near Shepherd's Chapel Mon last, Joseph Barthell Sr, formerly of the state of New York.

D near Federalsburg Sun last, Albert N. Davis.

DJ 5 Jan 1878/M at Dover 26th ult by Rev J. H. Caldwell, Dr. Theodore Saulsbury of Burrsville Md and Miss Hannah L. Brown of Dover Del.

M 19 Dec at the res of the bride's father by Rev Father Henchy, J. E. Reynolds of Talb and Annie E., eldest d/o W. W. Rhodes of QA Co.

DJ 12 Jan 1878/M 2nd inst at Bridgetown M.E. Church by Rev J. A. Brindell, Stephen R. Downes and Miss Emma C. Pippen, both of QA Co.

M 3rd inst at M.E. Parsonage Greensboro by Rev J. A. Brindell, Alex Butler and Miss Emma Moore, both of this county.

M on the 1st inst by Rev J. E. Smith, Azel Chaffinch and Miss T. J. Stevens, all of this county.

M at Zion M.P. Church near Federalsburg 25 Dec by Rev J. L. Kenney, George W. Pool of Caroline Co and Miss Emma V. Parker of Dorch Co.

M at the res of the bride's father 609 Lexington Ave New York City 2 Jan by Rev William H. Mickle, Oliver P. Davis s/o Hon. Curtis Davis of Federalsburg and Miss Emma A. McDougall.

M at the res of Mr. Carroll near Dover Bridge in this county 25 Dec by Rev George T. Tyler, Robert G. Barker and Miss Annie L. Carroll, both of this county.

M 3rd inst at the res of the bride's father's father, James B. Patton to Miss Alexine Taylor eldest d/o Perry D. Taylor.

DJ 19 Jan 1878/M at the M.E. Church in Federalsburg 8th inst by Rev L. Jewell, Edward C. Fields eldest s/o Hon Daniel Fields to Miss Annie Watkins d/o Capt W. H. Watkins of Federalsburgh.

M at New Hope 9th inst by Rev J. L. Kenney, William Pritchett and Miss Willie Bowdle, all of this county.

M at the res of the bride's father in Centreville 16 Jan by Rev C. W. Prettyman, George T. Purvis and Miss Lida B. Hopkins, both of QA Co.

M in Greensboro 16th inst by Rev J. A. Brindle, William L. Pritchett to Miss Sallie E. Spence, both of Denton.

M at the M.E. Parsonage Marydel 2 Jan by Rev E. H. Hynson, John R. Price and Miss Annie Steele, both of Kent Co Del.

DJ 26 Jan 1878/M in Balt 29 Nov, Walter Wyatt and Miss Willie M. Todd, both of Talb Co.

Newspaper Abstracts

DJ 2 Feb 1878//Editor comment: Many of the death notices had been clipped out
of the 1878 issues held by the Pratt Library, the only extant copies; however
a summary list of deaths occurring during 1878 are recorded in the Denton
Journal in the December 28th issue, extracted on page 46.

D at his res near Goldsboro in the 2nd election dist 15 Jan, Edward V. Morris
at 52 yrs of age.

DJ 9 Feb 1878/M on the 3rd inst in Wyoming M.E. Church by Rev D. W. C.
McIntre, James E. Ayers of this county and Miss Sallie Scott of Dover Del.

DJ 16 Feb 1878/M Mon afternoon 4 Feb in Presbyterian Church at Federalsburg
by Rev E. L. Bowing, Isaac W. Robinson and Miss Lydia E. Garrett.

M near Templeville 7 Feb by Rev E. H. Hynson, John W. Shewbrooks of Caroline
Co and Miss Annie Hall of QA Co.

DJ 23 Feb 1878/M near Easton 16 Feb by Rev D. R. Wright, James S. Willis of
Caroline Co and Miss Mary Shufelt of Talb Co.

DJ 9 Mar 1878/Mrs. Lane wife of Francis Lane res near Bridgetown d 28 Feb.

DJ 23 Mar 1878/D at the res of John Russell near Burrsville, John W. Vause in
the 77th yr.

M at the res of the bride's father in Tuckahoe Neck last Wed morning by Rev
J. E. Smith, Thomas W. Jones of New York and Miss Martha Furman.

DJ 18 May 1878/M Thurs evening 9 May at the res of E. J. Grant 1808 Montrose
Street by Rev T. Harrison, S. Thomas Jester of Phila and Miss Sallie A.
Shields of this town.

DJ 8 June 1878/M 28th ult at Wash D. C., Mr. W. E. Witherbee and Miss Mary
Maxwin, both of this county.

DJ 31 Aug 1878/D George Francis Beaven infant s/o George Hendley and Mary
Florence Beaven of Hillsboro Md 18 Aug age 11 mos and 14 das.

A colored man, Richard Jones, was drowned Mon afternoon at 3 o'clock at
Wayman's wharf on Tuckahoe Creek 2 miles below Hillsboro while pushing a scow
from the wharf to a schooner lying a short distance above.

DJ 28 Sep 1878/M at Bond Street M.E. Church in Balt Thurs night of last week,
C. H. Elliott to Miss Mollie Fountain.

DJ 26 Oct 1878/D Bessie Virginia 2nd d/o James W. and Grace A. Holt of
Hillsboro 5 Sep age 1 yr, 5 mos, 16 das.

DJ 16 Nov 1878/Luther M. Jewell s/o Luther W. and Julia A. Jewell was born 14
Nov 1865. On Fri evening while driving a mule which was geared to a cart the
mule became frightened and turning suddenly aside threw him out of the cart
inflicting a wound in the head from which he died the next day about one
o'clock P.M.

DJ 23 Nov 1878/M in Harrington 6th inst by Rev A. W. Milby, James W. Blades
of Kent Co Del and Miss Sallie F. Jewell of Tuckahoe Neck.

DJ 30 Nov 1878/M in Dover 20th inst by Rev John Ervin, William Driggis and
Miss Sarah Pearce, both of this county.

M on the morning of the 28th at the res of the bride's father by Rev J. E.
Smith, Richard T. Morgan and Miss Susie A. Ringold.

M in Kent Co Del 24 Nov by Rev A. D. Dick, Wheatley Travers and Miss Loulie
Harrington.

M 7 Dec at the res of the bride's father, Daniel C. Adams on the evening of the 4th inst by Rev J. E. Smith, Gootee S. Liden of Caroline Co and Miss Nancy H. Adams of Sussex Co Del.

DJ 28 Dec 1878/The following are the names and dates of the deaths that have occurred in this county since the first of last January. These include all that have been reported to the JOURNAL.

January: 1st, John Palmer, 50; 2nd, John H. Russum, 80; 7th, Miss Mary Fearns, 74; 8th, Mr. Darling Rash, 65; 8th, S. A. E. Hackett, 15; 6th, William Staton, 7; 26th,in Columbia, S. C., Mrs. Loretto West, 72.

February: 23rd, Grace Bishop, 15 mos; 19th, Mrs. Elizabeth Hinson, 80; 11th, Joseph Everngam; 19th, Mrs. Sarah Beachamp; 26th, in Balt, Sydney Robertson, infant s/o Samuel and Mary E. Fountain; 20th, John Bradley, 75; 9th, Allie Wilson, about 15 mos; 15th, Thomas C. Wyatt, 60; 13th, Edgar Plummer, 64; 19th, Jeremiah Beachamp, 63; 28th, John Collison, about 94; 26th Mr. Daker Booker 74.

March: 3rd, Mrs. Margaret Andrew; 3rd, Levin Butler; 9th, John W. ___; Martha P. Cover, 18; 12th, Mrs. Sallie A. Stephens, 43; 10th, Rev W. C. Ames, D. D. S., 39; 19th, QA Co, James J. Williams, 82; 27th, Vienna, Bessie V. Shewbrooks, 5; 22nd, at Wye Mills, Thomas Harold Saulsbury, 18 mos.

April: 25th, near Preston, Harry Field Douglass.

May: 27th, Mrs. Mary Eaton, 33.

June: 5th, Henry F. Chaffinch, 3 mos; 7th, Emma Smith, 8; 9th, Miss Annie Porter, 17; 15th, Mrs. Elizabeth A. Jump, 100; 17th, Charles W. Hignutt, 19; 16th, Thomas Jacobs Wright, 16; 2nd, Fisher Collins, 24; 30th, Mrs. Margaret A. Wright.

July: 9th, John Calvin Thawley, 13 mos; 15th, Mamie C. Dixon, 16; 18th, Frisby Ewell, 78; 21st, James Wix, 16, at Stone River Cal., Samuel Anthony, formerly of this county, 76; 23rd,Miss Annie M. Livingston, 23.

August: 5th, Mrs. Elizabeth Faulkner, 27; 1st, at Ocean City, J. Boon Reyner, 35; 21st, Richard C. Webber, 18; 12th, Mrs. Elizabeth Towers, 51; 22nd, Olive Harris, 12; 18th, George Francis Beaven, 11 mos; 11th, Jefferson Stewart, 17; 22nd, Mollie E. Davis, 19; 26th, George Conoway Chambers, 8.

September: 3rd, Mrs. Margaret Rowins, 75; 5th, Mrs. Sallie Cheezum, 19; 9th, Susie Kinnamon, 17; 6th, Estelle Fletcher, 16 mos; 8th, Mrs. Elizabeth Hubbard 64; 10th, Maurice Wright Ridgely, infant; 22nd, Laura V. Matthews, 14; 5th, Bessie Virginia Holt, 17.

October: 8th, Enous Alfred Wright, 3.

November: 1st, Hannah Whiteside, 9; 6th, Mrs. Louisa Glaser; 16th, Martin Robinson, 96; 24th, Andrew J. Willoughby, 20; 24th, near Wooden Hawk Del, Mrs. Jacob Patton.

December: 5th, Howard S. Hobbs, infant.

M on the morning of the 24th inst at the res of the bride's father near Potters Landing by the Rev J. E. Smith, G. Lacy Stevens and Miss Allie Williamson d/o Elias W. Williamson.

Killed instantly - Samuel Bouchell whilst assisting in shifting some cars at North East Md last week, was caught beneath a falling car which toppled over and fell on one side of the track killing him instantly. J. W. Campbell was also considerably hurt by the same accident.

There have been 83 marriages licenses since the first of the year.

Willie s/o the late Charles W. Greenly, about fifteen yrs of age who lives with his widowed mother two miles east of Greensborough, was fearfully burned by falling into the fire in an open fire-place during an epileptic fit on Mon afternoon last. His mother left him only for a few minutes to go to the smoke house, when hearing the cry that precedes a fit of the kind it alarmed her and she rushed back and found that the child had fallen backward into the fire. The screams of the mother upon discovering him brought to her aid an older son who snatched him from the ...

M on 18 Dec at St. Pauls M.E. Church by Rev E. H. Miller, Charles H. Fleming of Caroline Co and Miss Ella Jackson.

M on the evening of the 24th inst at Shepherd's M.E. Chapel by Rev J. E. Smith, Alexander Russel and Miss Laura Stafford.

M by Rev A. D. Dick on the 19th, Jacob S. Kenney and Harriett A. Carre.

M by Rev A. D. Dick 23 Dec, Samuel P. Quillen and Mary P. Butler.

M on the evening on the 26th inst at the res of the bride's father near Denton by Rev James Rich, Noah J. Williams and Miss Mary E. Roe.

D in this town Sun last after a lingering illness of typhoid fever, John R. Morgan, about 35 yrs of age.

DJ 4 Jan 1879/Mr. R. S. Farnum a gentleman from Pennsylvania who bought the Isaac Mason farm near Ruthsburg and has been living in Hillsborough for four months until he could get possession of the farm on the 1st inst was kicked in this stable by a strange horse on Fri 27th ult. At 3 o'clock Sun morning he died. He leaves a wife and no children. (A long item.)

M at Thawleys Chapel in Tuckahoe Neck Thurs evening 2 Jan by Rev J. E. Smith, Dr. Charles R. Straughn of Centreville and Miss Tina Anderson d/o the late Stephen H. Anderson.

M 2 Jan at Thawley's Chapel by Rev A. D. Dick, John M. Seward of QA Co and Miss Anna Anderson.

M by Rev W. W. Watts, Reynor B. Downes and Frances E. Coursey.

DJ 11 Jan 1879/M on the evening of d Dec 3rd ult at the res of the bride's mother in Henderson by the Rev Farland, Mr. F. B. Sweeney and Miss Annie Reed.

M at the Presbyterian Church in Federalsburg 26 Dec ult by Rev E. L. Boing, Mr. L. Trice and Miss Nellie Stevenson d/o Thomas Stevenson formerly of Birmingham England, all of this county.

M at Bethel M.E. Church Tues evening 31 Dec by Rev William Harris, Webster Kinder of Sussex Co Del to Miss Addie Waters of Caroline Co.

M at the M.E. Church Tues evening 2 Jan by J. W. Carroll, H. C. Horner and Miss Mary Hollyday, all of Caroline Co.

M at Burrsville 7th inst by Rev A. D. Dick, Isaac Harris and Marcelene Nutter.

M in Easton on the 2nd by Rev D. R. Wright, Sylvester F. Andrew and Miss Anna E. Pritchett, both of Caroline Co.

M on 8th inst at the res of the bride's father in Denton by Rev J. E. Smith, Mr. W. E. Hubbard and Miss Mollie Lednum.

M at St. Pauls Church Hillsborough by Rev Beaven 24th ult, W. Hunter of QA Co and Millie R. Barwick, formerly of Balt.

M Tues last by Rev G. F. Beaven, Ortera Hubbard and Miss Constance L. Simpson, all of this county.

M 8th inst by Rev J. E. Smith at Concord M.E. Church, Francis A. Clark and Miss Wilmina Todd, all of this county.

M on the 8th inst at M.E. Church Denton by Rev J. E. Smith, John Bloxon and Miss Belle Collison, all of this county.

D near Ruthsburg 1 Jan of pneumonia, Darius Montague, formerly of this county, 42 yrs of age.

D at Cordova Mon night 30 Dec, Solomon Pippin Sr, formerly of this county, age about 60 yrs.

DJ 18 Jan 1879/M in St. Pauls Chapel Hillsborough 24 Dec by Rev George F. Beaven, Michael Lambert and Miss Elenora Casin, both of Talb Co.

M 8th inst at St. Johns Church in Phila, John Lupton of Phila and Miss Josephine Lockerman, formerly of this place.

M 12th inst by Rev A. D. Dick, Thomas Sipple and Miss Roxanna Voss, all of Del.

M Wed 15th inst at Hyattsville M.E. Church, South, by Rev W. H. D. Harper, Robert S. Fountain of Easton and Miss Clara D. Carlton d/o H. L. Carlton of the "Highlands" Prince Georges Co.

D in Federalsburg 8th inst, Claudia infant d/o John and Ann Jennings, age 1 yr and 7 mos.

DJ 25 Jan 1879/M 14th inst by Rev J. L. Kenney, Asbury Wright of Dorch Co and Miss Kate Evans of Caroline Co.

M at Wesley's M.E. Chapel on the evening of the 22nd by Rev J. E. Smith, Peter W. Wright of Caroline Co and Miss Virginia R. Outten of Kent Co Del.

D at Federalsburg 13th inst James L. Thomas age about 30 yrs.

DJ 1 Feb 1879/M 19th ult in New York City, Henry Glaser of this county and Miss Rosa of New York.

D at Medford's Wharf 27 Jan at the res of Capt James T. Bowdle, Robert Walker in the 73rd yr.

DJ 8 Feb 1879/M on the evening of the 5th inst at the res of the bride's parents near Vernon by Rev J. E. Smith, James H. Ross and Miss Sarah E. Ward, all of Kent Co Del.

M 29 Jan at the res of the bride by Rev E. H. Miller, William H. Dean of Caroline Co and Miss Jennie Payne of Talb.

M Wed 29th ult at the res of the bride's parents in QA Co by Rev J. R. Dill, Wright Hall and Miss Lizzie Carson, both of Marydel Md.

M at the res of the bride's father 27 Jan by Rev James H. Rich, Willard C. Todd of this county and Miss Wilmina A. Willoughby of Sussex Co Del.

M 29th ult at Preston, Mr. F. J. Willoughby and Miss Adah M. Robinson, all of this county.

D in Davis Co Mo 22 Nov of lung fever, Benjamin F. Colescott in the 23rd yr.

Newspaper Abstracts

D 24th ult at her husband's res at Chestnut Woods Caroline Co, Mrs. Newton wife of William P. Newton age about 40 yrs.

DJ 15 Feb 1879/M 4th inst at the res of the bride's parents by Rev Albert Chandler brother-in-law of the bride, Mr. J. R. Woodall to Miss Ella N. d/o William L. Godwin of Crumpton.

D at his res in Greensborough Mon night last of paralysis, Andrew Baggs Sr age 61 yrs.

D at Templeville Wed of last week Mrs. W. Elliott age about 60 yrs.

D near Templeville Wed last Bernart s/o Charles Smith age about 4 yrs.

D Thurs morning the 13th inst at his res in Greensborough, William B. Massey in the 64th yr.

DJ 22 Feb 1879/M 18th inst in Bethlehem by Rev Daniel Wright, William J. Williamson and Miss Lizzie R. Knowles, all of Caroline Co.

M at Queenstown 19th inst by Rev Father Henchy, Louis Shafer and Mrs. Annie Barthell.

D near Coburn's Corner in this county Mon night last, Mrs. Louisa Coulburn, age about 60 yrs.

DJ 1 Mar 1879/M at the parsonage Trappe Talb Co Wed morning 26 Feb by Rev Charles Hill Presiding Elder, Joseph Mallalieu of this county and Miss Sallie Massey Warner d/o Rev William M. Warner of the Millington Conference.

DJ 8 Mar 1879/"Alex W. Gootee a former citizen of this county died of yellow fever at Rio de Janeiro on 25 January last after an illness of a few days. He left his home and friends here in the fall of 1874 on the three masted schooner George Churchman built at Greensborough and has followed the life of a sea man ever since. Last fall he was transferred to the barque Mary McKee and sailed for Rio at which port the captain and crew were afflicted with that fatal disease, yellow fever which terminated fatally to young Gootee. Captain Risley speaks in the highest terms of the deceased and his death is regretted by those of his shipmates. He was 23 years of age.-"

M by Rev A. D. Dick 27 Feb, Edward T. Cohee and Mrs. Mollie E. Sipple, all of Kent Co Del.

M by Rev A. D. Dick 5th inst, John W. Thawley and Mrs. Adlaiel E. Cochran, all of Kent Co Del.

D on the 21st ult at the res of Robert H. Smith, his son Leonard N. Smith, 12 yrs old.

The JOURNAL received a few days ago a letter inclosing a subscription from Joseph Satterfield, who left this county in 1835 and is now residing at Sames Valley, Jackson, Oregon. From the tone of his letter he seems to be prospering in his business affairs.

On Thrus last Dr. C. W. Williamson removed from Adamsville Del to the Dixon property in this town adjoining the P.E. Church.

DJ 22 Mar 1879/D at Goldsborough 14th inst in the 54th yr, William H. Breeden.

D near Burrsville 5th inst, Anna d/o John W. and Laura Morgan, age 1 yr, 5 das.

D near Bethlehem at the res of her uncle John A. Dillin on 13th inst, Ellen

Sophia Pratt age 21 yrs, 3 mos and 7 das. She "passed 15 yrs of her brief existence on a bed of suffering."

DJ 29 Mar 1879/M at the res of the bride's father 19 Mar by Rev S. B. Southerland D.D., Rev W. J. D. Lucas of the Maryland Annual Conference of the M. P. Church to Miss R. Annie d/o Samuel H. Fluharty of Preston.

D on the 26th inst at the res of her son-in-law James Beachamp, Mrs. Rebecca Lockerman wid of the late Richard Lockerman, about 82 yrs old.

D near Trenton N.J. at the res of his brother-in-law, Jacob Hendrickson, the Rev John Hough Presiding Elder of the Wilmington Conference of congestion of the brain in the 58th yr.

D near Union Grove 31 Mar, Mrs. Elizabeth Patchett in the 68th yr.

DJ 19 Apr 1879/M at Christ Church Denton Tues morning last by Rev Dr. E. J. Stearns, Dr. Enoch George and Miss Eva Horsey d/o William G. Horsey.

D in this place Fri last after a short illness, Miss Lizzie McKnett in the 57th yr.

D at New Hope in the 5th dist on the 4th inst, Daniel Alford, age 80 yrs.

D near Preston 13th inst William Wheelington age about 75 yrs.

DJ 26 Apr 1879/M 17th inst at the bride's res in Federalsburg by Rev J. W. Carroll, Washington Brewington and Mrs. Rhoda Magee.

M by Rev J. A. Brindle in the M.E. Church Greensboro on 16th inst, Mr. T. B. Pritchett and Mrs. Sarah M. Goodrich.

DJ 3 May 1879/M on the 24th ult at the res of the bride's father W. S. Goslin of Federalsburg by Rev J. P. Otis of Cambridge assisted by Rev W. B. Walton, Rev Isaac Jewell of the Wilmington Conference and Miss Annie M. Goslin.

D in Greensborough Wed 23 ult, Thomas J. Earrickson age about 78 yrs.

DJ 10 May 1879/D in Phila 30 Apr of compression of the brain, John Lupton age 30 yrs.

D in Centreville Sun afternoon last. Mrs. Susan J. Vane age 65 yrs.

DJ 17 May 1879/D at his res in Federalsburg Sun morning 4th inst, Jacob H Rhoads in the 67th yr.

D 20 Mar, Mrs. Annie Saulsbury w/o Robert Saulsbury.

DJ 24 May 1879/Married - Eugene M. Sanson and Miss Emma C. Roberts, according to rites of the Moravian Church 1 Jan by the Episcopalian services 15 May.

M 11 May at "Winkleton" by T. J. Slaughter, Bennett Gardner of Caroline Co to Laurel V. Jarrell of Talb.

M Wed 16 May by Rev J. E. Horney, James Breeding and Miss Roxanna Porter, all of this county.

D in the 2nd dist Fri last after a lingering illness, Mr. Moulten Plummer, age about 50 yrs.

DJ 31 May 1879/M 28th inst at Concord Church by Rev J. E. Smith, Charles Clark and Miss Ida Everngham.

DJ 7 Jun 1879/M at Easton M.E. Church 28th inst by Rev T. L. Tomkinson, Thomas L. Day of Caroline Co and Miss Catharine Pasterfield of Talb Co.

Newspaper Abstracts

D near Goldsboro 1 Jun of pneumonia, Miss Kate Morris, age 26 yrs.

D Fri morning 6 Jun, Mrs. Jane Medford wife of William W. Medford near Denton age 30 yrs and 16 das.

DJ 14 Jun 1879/D at his father's res near Whitleysburg Fri 6th inst, Calvin Cooper s/o John W. Cooper, age about 26 yrs.

D at his res near Preston Sun last after a protracted illness, Jesse Hubbard, age about 70 yrs.

D Fri 6th inst near Hillsboro, Edward Holliday about 50 yrs old.

DJ 28 Jun 1879/M in Camden Del 19th inst by Rev Joseph Robinson, Alexander W. Jones and Miss Lizzie Anderson, both of Henderson Md.

D 28 Apr at the res of Mr. J. T. Hynson in Wilmers Neck QA Co, Mrs. Ann Straughn, age about 86 yrs.

D at his res Sun 6 Apr, John Reid age 54.

DJ 5 Jul 1879/D in Kent Co Del 28 Apr, William Gullett formerly of this county, age 64.

D 4th inst near Burrsville of consumption, Mrs. Sallie Blades, age about 20.

D Sat 28th ult, Mrs. A. Towers.

DJ 12 Jul 1879/M at the res of the bride's father, Edward Adams of this county 1 Jul,by Rev E. Boing, Benjamin F. Williams of Federalsburg and Miss Tryphena Adams.

M at the M.E. parsonage in this town Thurs last by Rev J. E. Smith, Thomas A. Kennard formerly of QA Co and Miss Lina Lane, all of this county.

D near Concord 27 Jun, Mrs. Sarah B. Dukes, age about 40.

D in Washington 5th inst after a prolonged illness, Rev William M. Boynton formerly a res of this county near Potters Landing.

D in Federalsburg 28 Jun of emphysema of the lungs, Mrs. Elizabeth Willoughby wife of Richard J. Willoughby and d/o the late Newton Andrew of Caroline Co, in the 49th yr.

DJ 19 Jul 1879/D Sun last near Concord, John Wilson of consumption, age about 55 yrs.

DJ 26 Jul 1879/A dispatch from New York on the 22nd inst conveys to us that on that day Mr. Horace E. Wilson, a resident of Ridgely, formerly engaged as entry clerk in the office of the Merchants Dispatch Transportaion Company of that city, fell from a fifth story window upon an extension roof of the building. He settled in Ridgely only a short time ago as a real estate agent.

DJ 16 Aug 1879 / We are pained to announce the death of the Hon. William A. Ford which took place on Tuesday last on the 12th inst at his late residence in Tuckahoe Neck from a protracted cold. Age 74 yrs. He had been a resident of Caroline Co since boyhood. He entered the office of Register of Wills as an apprentice in his twelfth year, George A. Smith being the encumbent. He succeeded James Sangston and became Register of Wills in the early part of 1832 and since then has been either Register of Wills or Judge of the Orphan's Court to the time of his death with the exception of about six years. His remains were interred on the Griffith farm near this town. (Two long items)

M in this place Wed 6 Aug by Rev James H. Rich, Thomas J. Eaton and Miss Mary J. Allen, all of this county.

M 14th inst at the res of the bride's father in Tuckahoe Neck, Selby Smith and Miss Alice Green.

D near Burrsville Thurs last, Mrs. Baker wife of Shadrack Baker, age about 35 yrs.

D near Andersontown Fri last, James Thawley age 66 yrs and 47 yrs a member of the M.E. Church.

D at Henderson Tues the 5th inst Winfred s/o William L. and Sarah A. Pritchett age 7 mos and 23 das.

D at the res of the late Thomas Jones 10 Aug, Miss Sarah M. Jones.

DJ 23 Aug 1879/ Col. Stephen J. Bradley a native of this county but for 40 years a prominent citizen of Queen Anne's county died Thursday the 14th inst at his residence, Cottage Hill, in the 71st year of his age. His biography we take from the Centreville Observer. Col. Bradley was born in Caroline Co 17 Dec 1808. His father John Bradley, a farmer, d in Tuckahoe Neck in 1820. His mother was Rebecca Jump d/o Benjamin Jump of that county. She was a devoted member of the M.E. Church and an exemplary wife and mother. She d 1818 when her son Stephen was only 10 yrs old. In 1834 Col. Bradley removed to QA Co settling near Hillsborough and in 1842 removed to "Cottage Hill," which estate he owned and operated to the present. He m 19 Jun 1828 Miss Maria F. Baynard d/o Daniel Baynard of Caroline Co who at her death left five children, one of which d in 1848. After the death of his first wife he m her sister, Elizabeth who with her two daughters survive him. (Additional information given on his political career.)

Mr. B. H. Harrington of the Easton bar has gone to Kansas City and expects to settle there in practice of his profession.

M 11 Aug at the res of the bride by Rev J. E. Nicholson, Benjamin Fleming of Harrington Del and Mrs. Mary A. Flowers of Sussex Co Del.

M at the res of the bride's father 5 Aug near Wrights Cross Roads by Rev W. R. McFarlane, Charles G. Ross and Miss Amanda Jones, all of Kent Co Del.

D near Federalsburg 14th inst after a protracted illness, Mrs. IsaacC. Fleetwood.

D in this town 13th inst of cholera infantum, David Lorenzo infant s/o D. L. and Sidney A. Cline Balt City, age 1 yr, 4 mos, 9 das.

DJ 30 Aug 1879/A reunion of the family of Kenley Wright took place at Hurlock's campground in Dorch Co.

DJ 6 Sep 1879/Centreville is having a first class social sensation. The wid of the late George W. Taylor formerly of this county was engaged to be married to one J. W. Merchant the superintendent of her estate and Thurs evening of last week was the time appointed for the wedding. From Thurs until the following Sun she remained closely confined to her room and Sun evening disappeared.

M 2 Sep at the M.E. Parsonage in Denton by Rev J. E. Smith, Frederick N. Snell and Miss Belle Carter.

M at the res of Mr. H. J. Halesman near American Corner 20 Aug by Rev Payne, Alfred W. Trice of Federalsburg and Mrs. Sarah W. Walker, late of England.

D in New York Aug 22nd, James McGregor of Caroline Co, clerk in the employment of M. W. Goldsborough, Paymaster U.S.N., age 38 yrs.

D near Morgan's Mill 25 Aug, Charles Herbert infant s/o M. L. and Sarah J. Sullivan, age 11 mos.

D Sun 31 Aug at the res of Mrs. Annie Shields in this place, Lillie d/o S. T. and Sallie A. Jester, age 5 mos and 4 das.

DJ 13 Sep 1879/M at William Willey's near Andersontown 12 Aug by Rev A. D. Dick, Robert H. Meloney and Jody V. Beachamp, all of Caroline Co.

DJ 20 Sep 1879/A colored boy named George Roberts of QA Co whilst crabbing last week fell overboard and drowned.

DJ 27 Sep 1879/On Thursday last the wife of George Collins who res near Farmington met with a terrible accident which has since terminated fatally. Mrs. Collins was engaged in washing and while attempting to put some clothes in a wash boiler which was standing on a fire built in the yard, her dress ignited and she was almost instantly enveloped in flames. She lingered until Sunday afternoon when she passed peacefully away.

DJ 4 Oct 1879/Walter Bradley a highly esteemed young man of this town left yesterday the 22nd for Shelbyville, Shelby Co, Mo. Friends wish him abundant success in his new home.

D Wed last at his res, Capt James Passapae age 67 yrs.

DJ 11 Oct 1879/James C. Murphy d near Union Grove M.P. Church in the 4th dist 30 Sep age about 84 yrs.

DJ 18 Oct 1879/D 13 Sep, Edward Dabson, of consumption, in the 63rd yr.

D suddenly at Greensboro Tues 7th inst, Mr. Crosby, at an advanced age, formerly of Kent Co Md.

D near Bethlehem 13 Sep, Willie only s/o Mrs. Maggie and the late James M'Gregor U.S.N., age 9 mos and 19 das.

DJ 25 Oct 1879/M at the M.E. Church at Greensboro 16 Oct by Rev J. A. Brindle, Edward W. Greeves of Wilmington Del and Miss Laura Simpers of Greensboro.

D near Greensboro 13 Oct Ennalls Hubbard, age 75 yrs.

D on 8th inst in Anderstntown of congestion of the brain, Francis H. Cannon oldest s/o Henry H. and Martha W. Cannon, age 21 yrs, 5 mos, 2 das.

D Tues 14 Oct in Greensboro, Eliza A. Case wife of Capt T. D. Case, age 64 yrs less 5 das. Balt and Phila papers please copy.

DJ 15 Nov 1879/The wife of Robert Johnson of Farmington Del rushed in front of a down train on the Delaware Railroad and was fattally injured but was able to tell bystanders that the devil told her to do it.

Purnell Fleetwood formerly of this county son of William Fleetwood of Tuakahoe Neck and now res at Waverly Station Va, has been visiting relatives and friends. He is doing a prosperous mercantile busines.

About 9 o'clock at night Tues last Thomas Fields foruth s/o the Hon. Daniel Fields of Caroline Co was found mortally wounded in a swamp, within sight of home, by a shot gun. He d Wed morning. (A long article describing the circumstances of his death)

M in Easton Tues 11 Oct by Rev T. L. Tomkinson, William P. Chaffinch, formerly of this county and Miss Annie A. Hull of Easton.

DJ 29 Nov 1879/Dr. Lewis Chaplain, a promising young physician of Trappe d last Sun of consumption.

M in Federalsburgh 13th inst by Rev W. B. Walton, Albert J. Jennings of Baldwin's Theatre, San Francisco and Miss Catharine R. Mowbray d/o the late Alfred Mowbray of Federalsburg.

M on the 27th inst at the res of the bride's father in Denton by Rev Robert W. Todd, P.E. Dover Dist, assisted by Rev J. E. Smith, Charles W. Emmerich and Miss Lizzie E. Jump d/o the Hon. Robert J. Jump.

M in this town 26th inst at the res of John R. Fountain by Rev James H. Rich, Charles W. Smith and Miss Christiana Wright.

M at Hobbs Wed 26 Nov by Rev J. E. Horney, Jesse Dukes and Miss L. Arena Hitch, all of this county.

D 12 Nov after an illness of 4 mos, Emily A. Sherwood, age 76 yrs, 27 das.

D in Federalsburg Fri 14th inst of typhoid pneumonia, Mrs. Jane Fleetwood wife of John T. Fleetwood, age 54 yrs.

D in Greensborough Mon 17th inst of diptheria in the 6th year of his age Turpin Moore s/o the late Henry and Mary Ellen Horsey of Greensborough and grandson of Rev G. W. Kennedy.

D in Balt City Thurs evening last Robert Howard infant s/o Robert H. and Regina D. Jones age 6 mos and 20 das.

D on the 10th inst at Hillsborough, Clyde only s/o Garretson and Mollie E. Smith, age 11 mos and 17 das.

DJ 6 Dec 1879/Henry Mullikan an elderly invalid of Centreville shot himself through the heart.

D in Easton 3rd inst Robert H. Colescott former res of this county in the 47th yr of his age.

D at East New Market Dorch Co Mon 24th inst, Francis M. Hubbard of Hunting Creek, Caroline Co, age about 45 yrs.

DJ 20 Dec 1879/Mr. Joseph S. Daily s/o John Daily, County Commissioner was m Wed 2 P.M. to Miss Bell Emerson near Slaughter's Del. After the ceremony which took place at Thomas J. Marvel's, the bride's grandfather....

M in Ridgely on the 18th inst by Rev Joseph Hannaberry, George W. Bowers to Miss Permilla Lesnett, both of Caroline Co.

D in Bolinbroke Neck, Trappe Dist 15th inst of cronic croup, Annie Adelaine 3rd d/o Solomon J. and Addie McMahan, age 4 yrs, 11 mos, 6 das.

DJ 27 Dec 1879/M at the M.E. Church in Denton Tues evening 23 Dec by Rev J. E. Smith assisted by Rev L. E. Smith, John E. Wilson of Tuckahoe Neck and Miss Ida Downes d/o Hon. William H. Downes of Denton. The reception was given by her brother, P. W. Downes.

M at the res of the bride's parents 10th inst by Rev S. S. Hepbron of St. Paul's P.E. Church, J. W. Beachamp formerly of Caroline Co and Miss Lida C. Brannock of Kent Co.

M at Schaghticoke Hill, N.Y. by Rev James B. Wood, William B. Medford formerly of Denton and Miss Mary A. Eckner, both of Valley Falls N.Y.

D in Federalsburg 18th inst of enteritis, Willis Charles eldest s/o the late Hon. Jacob Charles in the 69th year of his age. Willis Charles was recently appointed clerk to the county commissioners. From his early boyhood he res in Federalsburg.

Newspaper Abstracts

DJ 10 Jan 1880/M at Burrsville Md 6 Jan by Rev A. D. Dick, George W. Harris and Miss Annie Lister.

M 16th inst by Rev Rich, William Payne and Miss Mary V. Marshall, all of Caroline Co.

M on the 23rd inst at the M.E. Parsonage in Federalsburg by Rev W. B. Walton, Thomas H. Butler and Miss Mary E. Dean d/o Elisha Dean of Caroline Co.

M Tues evening 31 Dec at Busie's M.E. Church by Rev J. R. Dill, Samuel Tarbutton of Henderson and Miss Sarah E. Emerson d/o Samuel Emerson of Ingleside QA Co.

D Mon 29 Dec at the res of J. B. Bishop of Hillsborough after a long illness, Charles S. Smith, age 24 yrs.

M on the 23rd at the res of Willis Noble near Preston by Rev W. B. Walton, George M. Taylor s/o Perry Taylor of Caroline Co and Miss Mary E. Wright d/o Rev D. R. Wright.

DJ 17 Jan 1880/James Barnes of Dublin dist Somerset Co d a few days ago from burns. (A long item.)

M at Templeville 16th inst by Rev Purdy, Stephen Spry Andrews of Dorch Co and Miss Nellie Paxson of Phila.

M at the res of the bride's father in Farmington 13 Jan by Rev Edwards, Edward N. Russell and Miss Mary Fisher d/o S. Fisher.

M on the 14th inst at the Concord M.E. Church by Rev J. E. Smith, T. Fred Garey and Miss Annie E. Dixon d/o James A. Dixon.

M 30 Dec at the bride's res by Rev James H. Rich, Charles H. Hignutt and Miss Eliza J. Trice, all of this county.

M 31 Dec by Rev J. H. Rich, William Robinson and Miss Jennie Wilson, all of this county.

M in Miles River Neck by Rev F. T. Tagy 6 Jan, Capt Greenbury Marshall Jr and Kate Hancock, all of Talb Co.

D near Federalsburg 5th inst, Miss Sallie Nichols, age 69 yrs.

DJ 24 Jan 1880/Dr. William D. Noble d suddenly at his res in Federalsburg at 11 o'clock P.M. last Sun of apoplexy in the 50th yr. He was a native of Delaware but early in his life moved to Federalsburg. For a number of years he was editor of the Federalsburg Courrier at the same time having a very large practice in his profession.

Houston Branch area - A Very distressing accident occured near Brown's saw mill a short time ago. A little child of James Southerlains caught fire and before assistance could be given was burned to death.

M at St. Pauls P.E. Church Wed 14th inst by Rev George F. Beaven, Charles Rathel of Talb Co and Miss Belle Jump d/o Robert J. Jump of Denton who gave away the bride. He was accompanied by his daughters and son-in-law, C. W. Emmerich.

M at the res of S. H. Fluharty 26 Dec by Rev W. J. D. Lucas, Mr. W. E. Eaton and Miss Margaret Williamson.

M at the res of the bride's father 14 Jan by Rev W. J. D. Lucas, Mr. W. H. Cohee and Miss Mary J. Smith.

Newspaper Abstracts

M at Preston M.E. Church 14 Jan by Rev W. J. D. Lucas, Thomas F. Eaton and
Miss Maggie Lang.

M at the res of the bride's father 15 Jan by Rev W. J. D. Lucas, Mr. C. W.
Fluharty and Miss Susan I. Turner.

M on the 22nd inst at the res of the bride's parents near Templeville by Rev
J. E. Smith, Charles P. Jump and Miss Emma Temple d/o John W. Temple.

D near Burrsville Wed 14th inst of consumption, Hester A. Dill, age about 53.

D in Greensborough 21st inst, Florence d/o James and Josephine Massey, age
about 4 yrs.

DJ 31 Jan 1880/M at Hobbs Wed 14 Jan by Rev J. E. Horney, John Pepper and
Miss Emma Ferrings, all of this county.

M the 21st inst at Bethlehem by Rev D. R. Wright, John W. Thomas and Miss
Sarah M. Williamson, all of this county.

M at the res of the bride's mother 13 Jan by Rev J. E. Smith, Capt Azeb T.
Hutchinson and Miss Mary C. Passapae d/o late Capt J. M. Passapae, all of
this county.

D in Preston 26th inst, Mary Catharine d/o James H. and Mary E. Douglass,
age 2 yrs and 8 mos.

DJ 7 Feb 1880/M at the res of Capt T. C. Eaton at Cambridge 28 Jan by Rev
J. P. Otis, James Hubbard of Cambridge and Miss Grace Gootee of Caroline Co.

M at Washington M.E. Church 14 Jan by Rev W. F. Corkran, Arthur Hitch of
Dorch and Miss Fannie A. Corkran of Caroline Co.

D near Ridgely on the 2nd inst Miss __Dukes d/o Thomas Dukes about 21 yrs.

D near Vernon Del Wed the 27th of consumption, John Sharp, age about 45 yrs.

D at Bridgetown, Caroline Co 15 Dec of cardiac disease, Mrs. Serena Boon,
age 75 yrs. Dover papers please copy.

DJ 14 Feb 1880/Mrs. Jane Tibbitt the wife of Samuel Tibbitt of Harrington has
eloped with Joseph Hill, her husband's half-brother.

Martin Smith d at his res near Burrsville 7 Feb, age 67 yrs.

D near Whiteleysburg Del Mon 2 Feb, Jacob Welsh, age 80 yrs.

AU 19 Feb 1880/Uriah Tarbutton res near Centreville and s/o S. S. Tarbutton,
d last Sun of lock jaw. He accidently cut off the front portion of one of his
feet about a week or ten days ago while cutting wood and tetanus set in.

D near Oxford, Talb Co, Sat last, Mrs. Fanny Bell wife of Frank Bell age
about 40 yrs.

M at Zion M. P. Church 4 Feb by Rev W. J. D. Lucas, Michael W. Johnson and
Miss Josephine Hubbard, all of this county.

M at the Zion M. P. Church by W. J. D. Lucas 11 Feb, William D. James and
Miss Hattie A. Parvin.

M 11 inst at Free Tabernacle M.E. Church, Hoboken N.J. by Rev D. B. F.
Randolf assisted by Rev Dr. Strong, Jerome A. Davis s/o Hon Curtis Davis of
Federalsburg and Miss Jennie E. DeRonde, all of Hoboken N.J.

M Tues evening 7th inst by Rev J. E. Smith, Capt Joseph Passapae and Miss
Amanda Roe, all of this county.

Newspaper Abstracts

AU 26 Feb 1880/Col. Hansan of Kent Co, lawyer, editor and author, d Fri last week in the 50th yr.

Dr. Benjamin F. Gootee d at his res in Smyrna Sat last in his 49th yr. He had a great many firends in this county.

At the last Quarterly Conference of Denton circuit the following ladies were appointed a committee on parsonage for the ensuing conference year: Denton, Mrs. Sarah Pearson and Mrs. Ida Wilson; Potters Landing, Mrs. Elias Williamson; Concord, Mrs. William Morgan; Bloomery, Mrs. D. Adams; Sheppards, Mrs. Downes Cranor; Wesley's Chapel, Mrs. Ferdinand Baynard; Harris' Chapel, Mrs. Josephine Downes.

D at the res of her father in Federalsburg 23rd inst after a short illness, Anna Jewell, age 35 yrs, wife of Rev I. Jewell of Wilmington Conference and d/o William S. and Catharine Goslin.

DJ 28 Feb 1880/M at the res of L. H. Fluharty 18th inst by Rev W. J. D. Lucas, James P. Karschner and Miss Annie Davis, all of Dorch Co.

M at the res of the bride 18 Feb by Rev A. A. Fisher, William T. Andrew and Miss Sallie E. Baker, both of Caroline Co.

AU 4 Mar 1880/On Mon last a boy named Kirk and a young man named Kurd were playing with an old pistol at Marydel when by some means the pistol was discharged sending a bullet into the brain of young Kirk, killing him almost instantly. Dr. James R. McClyment was sent for but the boy was dead before he could get there. He was about 14 yrs old.

David Gibbs, colored man, res near Marydel who was subject to epilepsy for some years got up and went down stairs a few nights since and while sitting in a chair was seized with a fit and fell into the fire burning himself horribly before he was discovered. Dr. McClyment was sent for. In a few days symptoms of tetanus supervened and Dr. Evans of Templeville was called in for consultation but all that medical skill could do was unavailing and he died of traumatic tetnus.

On Mon evening last about dusk as Frank Ayres was driving toward his home in Tuckahoe Neck and when near the res of George W. Richardson his horse was frightened, became unmanageable and ran away. At the turn in the road Mr. Ayres was thrown from his carriage and became entangled in the reins or wheels. He was dragged some seventy yards on the hard road before becoming detached, where he was shortly afterward found by Rev Young in an unconscious condition. The neighbors were alarmed and Mr. Kirkman and Mr. Urry removed Mr. Ayres to his home where he received medical attention. He regained consciousness in about two hours and fortunately no bones were broken. He was however badly bruised and lacerated. The horse ran on toward home and the carriage was completely wrecked.

Preston Letter - The wheat crop in this locality is looking remarkably well. Willis Wright in Poplar Neck has the finest field in the neighborhood as I have seen though Stephen Gifford is not far behind him and William R. Smook's field is also very promising.

Robert Todd was arraigned before Esquire Williamson Mon, in charge of Constable Rumbold, for committing an assault on his wife.

D in Galestown this county Mon 23 Feb, Cora F. E. wife of John E. Nichols, 22 yrs of age.

D near Concord 20 Feb, Mrs. Frances Covey, age 25 yrs.

Newspaper Abstracts

D after a brief illness of diptheric croup, Bessie youngest d/o Trustin and Annie E. Pippin, age 2 yrs, 5 mos, 15 das.

DJ 6 Mar 1880/D in Cambridge Sun 29 Feb at the res of her nephew Joseph Bradshaw, Miss Elizabeth Bradshaw, age 83 yrs.

AU 11 Mar 1880/James Hignutt near 80 yrs of age and for more than 40 yrs crier of the Circuit Court for this county, is confined to his room suffering from the dropsy.

Preston festival - Held by the Union Grove congregation in the new academy. ...a cake to one of the ladies (single) who received the most ballots at five cents each that evening among their friends. The ladies were: Miss Lizzie Willoughby of Union Grove, Miss Jennie Pritchett of Preston, Miss Ora Gale of Preston, Miss Susie Laing of Bethlehem and Miss Pheno Coulbourn of Zion.

The latest sensation is the elopement of Miss Annie M. Gibson and Harry W. Hynson (the silent man or better known perhaps as being the legal advisor of Judge Bond in the Hackett vs whiskey case). They were m 4 Mar by Rev William H. McFarlane.

M 2nd inst by Rev J. Hannaberry at the home of the bride, Quintus Hornbogen and Miss Ella Wiley, both of this county.

M 27 Jan at the res of the bride's father, Robert H. Jump by the Rev P. T. Warren, Daniel H. Cox of Caroline and Miss Clara E. Jump of Talb Co.

D in Hillsborough of consumption, Mary E. Wheeler wife of Capt C. C. Wheeler in the 33rd yr.

D at the res of Mr. Silverthorn in Greensboro Sat last after a long illness, Richard Bonn, formerly of Balt City, born 4 Oct 1808, d 6 Mar 1880.

D near Sheppard's Chapel Sat last after a long illness, Mrs. Angelina Cranor wife of William A. Cranor, age about 30 yrs.

D in Spaniard's Neck QA Co 17 Feb, Martha C. d/o J. T. Hynson, age 7 yrs, 3 mos, 5 das.

DJ 13 Mar 1880/D after a one-week illness, Ida V. d/o William T. Price on 7 Mar, age 9 yrs and 8 mos.

D in Preston 3rd inst at the res of W. S. Bradley, Mrs. Matilda Hopkins, age 78 yrs.

D 10th inst at Ridgely, an infant d/o Thomas A. Smith.

AU 18 Mar 1880/J. Hopkins Tarr, a prominent lawyer of Salisbury, d at his res in this place Thurs last. Born in Easton, he practiced law in Salisbury for a short time in 1847, having married Miss Sallie Rock, a step-daughter of Shiles C. Seabrease, who survives him. He then came to Denton and practiced his profession until 1863 when he returned to Salisbury and has since remained. He was a member of the constitional convention of 1867.

M 3rd inst by Rev D. R. Wright, Mr. D. R. Cheezum and Miss Maria P. Collins, all of this county.

M on the 10th inst by Rev D. R. Wright, Thomas Taylor and Miss Annie M. Williams, all of this county.

AU 25 Mar 1880/Frank Henry, colored servant of Dr. Alexander Hardcastle d of consumption 17th inst.

Mrs. Lowndes wife of Commodore Charles Lowndes d at his res on Miles River last Wed night. Mrs. Lowndes was a sister of the late Col. Edward Lloyd and also to Mrs. Commodore Buchanan and Mrs. William T. Goldsborough of Dorch, both of whom survive her. She was well advanced in yrs.

John L. White age 18 s/o Robert White a farmer living near Frankford, Sussex Co, was killed Wed by the upsetting of a cart he was driving to get a load of fire wood. The body of the cart becoming detached from the wheels and falling upon him, crushed his skull.

M near Marydel 2 Mar by Rev W. R. McFarlane, John Flemeing and Miss Ella Foreacres, both of this county.

M at Marydel by Rev W. R. McFarlane 2 Mar, William H. Carlyle and Miss Florence Moore, both of Kent Co Del.

M at the M.E. Parsonage Marydel by Rev W. R. McFarlane, Henry W. Hynson and Miss Annie M. Gibson, both of this county, on 11 Mar. (Note conflict with earlier item.)

M at the M.E. Parsonage Marydel by Rev W. R. McFarlane, James M. Stafford and Miss Hannah Faulkner, both of this county.

D Sat 13 Mar of diptheria, Freddie s/o Moses McCullough, age about 5 yrs.

AU 1 Apr 1880/M Tues evening 25 Mar at the res of the bride's uncle near Seaford Del by Rev T. A. Moore, Mr. E. H. S. James of Greensboro and Miss Lou D. Hopper.

M in Bethlehem 24 Mar by Rev D. R. Wright, John W. Gootee and Miss Amanda Marine, both of Dorch Co.

DJ 3 Apr 1880/Mrs. Lizzie Conaway wife of Robert Conaway of Preston was so badly burned Thurs evening of last week to cause her death Sat morning. The cause of the burning was the taking fire of her dress, from trimming the wick of a coal oil lamp while burning. The portion trimmed off was blazing and Mrs. Conaway intended to throw it upon the stove and did not know her mistake until her dress was blazing. Her little son Clayton aged 10 years was sleeping on the lounge in the room and as soon as he could be wakened bravely dashed water over his mother and extinguished the flames.

D   Frankie s/o Elisha A. and Eliza Lord of Landing Neck 19 Mar age 6 yrs, 1 mo, 11 das.

AU 8 Apr 1880/Mrs. Plummer of Talb Co whilst on her way to visit her daughter Mrs. Capt Start on Pacas Island last, met with an accident from which she died in a few hours.

A little son of William Stayton age about 5 yrs was drowned at Greensborough on Mon afternoon last. Mr. Stayton's res being located near the Choptank the little fellow strayed down along the river bank and fell into the water.

Mrs. Sallie Perry wid of the late Edward Perry and sister of Woodenhawk W. Ross of Del d in Easton Fri night last. She went to Easton to visit her daughter, Mrs. Franklin Davis and was attacked with pneumonia which proved fatal in a few days. She was 67 yrs old.

AU 15 Apr 1880/Mrs. Sallie F. Keating wife of Hon. Thomas J. Keating of QA Co d of congestive chill Mon afternoon last.

Jerry Cornish, an old colored man living in Meekins Neck Dorch Co, visited LeCompte's liquor store in the upper end of Lake's dist Mon evening after Easter and became very drunk. Later he was found drowned. (Long item)

AU 22 Apr 1880/Eliza Moore an insane colored woman was found dead in her cell in Cambridge jail last Fri morning.

M Thurs 8 Apr by Rev Loca, George T. Carter of Caroline Co and Miss Florence DeShields of Wash D. C.

M Tues evening 13 Apr at the M.E. Church South at Hillsborough, Fletcher Pennington to Miss Emma Thawley, both of This county.

D near New Hope, Caroline Co, Fri 9th inst, Minnie E. d/o John E. and Henritta Nichols, age 2 yrs, 10 mos, 27 das.

AU 29 Apr 1880/Robert Booker, one of the oldest citizens of the firs dist, d at his res at Goldsborough 19th inst, age 73.

D Fri 16th inst at the res of Foster Green near Andersontown of consumption, Miss Julia E. Brown, age 38 yrs.

D near Centreville Fri last after a brief illness, Mrs. Roxana Anderson wife of Isaac L. Anderson and d/o George W. Spurry of this county, age about 32 yrs.

AU 6 May 1880/Mrs. Sarah A. Wilson wife of John T. Wilson of Wilmington was buried at Greensboro Sat afternoon.

Mrs. Rachel M. Reynolds, mother of Joseph W. Reynolds and sister of the late Mrs. Jacob Tome, d at Port Deposit Fri last, age 69.

Samuel C. Brannock formerly of this county is a justice of the peace in Kent Co.

M 28th ult at the res of the bride's parents by Rev R. D. Bradley, William Tuff and Miss Lizzie Dean, both of this county.

M at "Ramsey" Talb Co 27 Apr by Rev G. H. Zimmerman, Rev John H. Davidson of Balt Conference M.E. Church South to Miss M. Augusta Jump d/o Hon. C. M. Jump.

D at Andersontown Mon 26th inst of consumption, Miss Emma Nuttle d/o Tilghman Nuttle.

DJ 8 May 1880/D at New Castle Me 28 Mar, Mary F. wife of Warren S.Jones, formerly of this county.

AU 20 May 1880/M on 6th inst at the res of the bride' parents by Rev Fisher, Stephen Fluharty and Miss Elizabeth E. Andrew, both of this county.

M Wed 12th inst at the res of the bride near Harrington Del by Rev J. E. Smith, William H. Deweese of Caroline Co to Mrs. Sarah Tinley.

AU 27 May 1880/James M. Vickers s/o the late Hon. George Vickers d in Chestertown last week of congestion of the brain in the 51st yr.

Mrs. Adelaide Hammond who was fatally burned in the Atlanta (Ga) Opera House last week was the d/o Andrew Coe who several years ago owned the Rich Neck Farm in Bay Hundred Talb Co and resides there.

D 14th inst a 10 year-old d/o Elijah Reed near Crumpton QA Co was burned to death by a exploding lamp.

Mr. James E. Caroll, principal of Greensboro Academy for a number of years past, was last week elected principal of the public schools at Dover Del. Mr. Caroll is a native of this county, born near Federalsburg and a graduate of Washington College.

M at the res of the bride's parents 13th inst by Rev James H. Rich, Major T. Cohee of Del and Miss Jennie Wooters of Caroline Co.

M 19th inst in Bethlehem by Rev D. R. Wright, Elijah M. Jester and Miss Julia Ann Legates, all of this county.

D in Miles River Neck Talb Co 11 May, John Hancock in the 53rd yr.

DJ 29 May 1880/Mr. J. P. Manlove of Greensborough is to remove to Oxford, having received an appointment of agent for the Delaware and Chesapeake Railray Co.

AU 3 Jun 1880/D in this town on Mon afternoon last after a long illness, James A. Fountain only s/o John R. Fountain, age 33 yrs, 3 das. He was for 8 mos a great sufferer from disease.

AU 10 Jun 1880/Mr. W. H. Lowe of Greensboro has been appointed inner guard at the House of Correction.

Joel Prettyman, father of Dr. J. S. Prettyman and grandfather of H. H. Prettyman, one of the editors of the Milford News, d at his home in South Milford about a week since, age 81 yrs.

D at his res in Tuckahoe Neck Mon last, Luther W. Jewell age 62 yrs.

D in Wilmington 7 Jun, Dr. E. T. Dunning.

William B. Lynch age 22 fell from the steamer Theodore Weems on an excursion from Balt to Cambridge and drowned near Poplar Island.

DJ 12 Jun 1880/Little Willie Hayward for-year old s/o Colonel Hayward of Easton was gored to death by a bull. (A long item.)

AU 17 Jun 1880/On Mon John Selby, colored, near Laurel, drowned.

On Fri afternoon last week Charles Swiggert met with an accident near Smyrna which resulted in his death on the following Sun; he was 13 yrs old.

John Melvin age 22, s/o Thomas Melvin of this place, who for several months past had been employed at the works of Jackson, Sharp and Co, Wilmington, on Sat morning last about one o'clock fell from the third story window of his sleeping room to the pavement below, a distance of about 25 feet. He d Sun morning about 4 o'clock. He had frequently been warned by his roommates of the danger of sleeping with his head partly out of the open window but he heeded not their warnings. His remains were interred at M.E. Churchyard in this place Tues last.

M Wed morning 9th inst by Rev G. F. Beaven, T. C. Stayton and Miss Mollie Williamson, all of Hillsborough.

M 9th inst at the res of the bride's father by Rev D. R. Wright, William Richard Carroll of Talb and Miss Josephine Cheezum of Caroline Co.

D 5th inst at his res near Henderson, William L. Reed, age 68 yrs.

D at his res in Del near Whiteleysburg on 23rd inst, Robert Greenlee, age 84 yrs and 6 mos. He leaves a widow, now 83 yrs old.

DJ 19 Jun 1880/M at the res of the bride's parents near Willow Grove Del on 7th inst by Rev J. R. Dill, A. C. Harris of Ohio and Miss Mary S. Dill.

D at the res of her husband of Diarrhea, Mrs. Nathaniel Butler, age 60 yrs.

AU 24 Jun 1880/D 15th inst at Ridgely, Raymond only s/o Luther and Hattie Whitby, age 8 mos.

AU 1 Jul 1880/Thomas Carmine s/o Thomas Carmine of Easton drowned at Deep Point near Easton, age about 11 yrs.

Newspaper Abstracts

M in Denton Tues 22 Jun by Rev Milby, Cropper T. White and Miss Annie M. Andrew, both of this county.

M in the M.E. Church South at Hillsboro 15 Jun by Rev G. H. Zimmerman, Thomas E. Davis and Miss Sarah A. Stewart.

D at the res of her husband near Preston 17 Jun, Mrs. Martha Ryan, age 21 yrs.

D near Harmony 16th inst of bilious dysentery, Nancy wife of James Butler in the 60th yr.

DJ 3 Jul 1880/D of Billious dysentery near Hillsborough 23 Jun, Bessie only d/o William and Lizzie Cahall, age 6 yrs and 6 mos.

AU 8 Jul 1880/William Wright, colored, was killed by a train on the track of the Eastern Shore Railorad.

DJ 10 Jul 1880/M on 4th inst at 8 o'clock P.M. at Bethel Church Caroline Co by Rev J. M. Elderice, James W. Thomas and Miss Alice Wyatt, both of Kent Co Del.

D on the 2nd inst near Smithville in the 72nd yr, David Favinger.

DJ 17 Jul 1880/Edward Dowling, a veteran nurseyman of the firm of Peters and Dowling who has superintended the Choptank nurseries below Denton for several yrs past, d at his res Tues last, age about 60 yrs. In 1851 he came to this country from England. He was engaged in Poeman's nursery in Massachussets for 10 yrs. He later went to California. He was buried in the Catholic burying ground in Denton.

Rev Samuel Sparklin a native of this county but since 1839 a res of Balt, d last Sat. He was born in Caroline Co 26 Jul 1800; joined the M.E. Church in 1820. He m Miss Rebecca Sullivan eldest d/o Peter Sullivan who resided in the neighborhood of Concord in 1821 and still survives him. He was untiring in the advocacy of the temperance cause in the old Washingtonian movement. Mr. Sparklin moved to Balt with his family in 1839. He had 16 children of whom 7 are living. (A long item)

M at Thawley's Wed evening last by Rev McLain, Marcus M Smith and Sallie M. Clark.

D after a long illness of consumption Sat 26 Jun, William T. Ringgold near Hillsborough.

DJ 24 Jul 1880/A white man, Samuel Hopkins, res on St. Peters Creek, Somerset Co, drowned last Thurs at the mouth of the Manokin River by upsetting of a skiff in which he was gathering the ores.

D in this town Mon evening last after a long illness, Mrs. Ann Newman, in the 67th yr.

DJ 7 Aug 1880/M at Thawley's Chapel Tues evening last by Rev Lane, Jacob Ghinger and Minnie V. Jewell, both of this county.

D Tues 3 Aug very suddenly, Annie d/o J. Hopkins of Greensborough, age about 6 yrs.

D Wed 4 Aug, Elizabeth wife of the late Samuel Hughes of Greensborough, age 77.

D at the res of Capt Robert Stewart near Denton Wed 4 Aug, Mrs. Nancy Pratt, age 78 yrs.

DJ 21 Aug 1880/D in Denton 17 Aug of cholera infantum, Marshall H. infant s/o Marshall S. and Lena Mutchler, age 8 mos and 2 weeks.

Newspaper Abstracts

DJ 28 Aug 1880/On Mon evening last about 6 o'clock Thomas P. Davis was found lying prostrate on his shop floor. He was a house carpenter; he had lived in Denton during the past 30 yrs. He leaves a wife and three children. For some yrs he had been an apoplectic and it's thought this caused his death.

James Hignutt, 80 yrs old, lacking one month and 10 das, d suddenly at his res about four miles below Denton Wed norning last at 6 o'clock. He res in Caroline Co all his life; he was crier of the court for 43 yrs.

D at Ruthsburg 19th inst of bilious dysentery, John M. Jones formerly of this county, in the 62nd yr.

DJ 11 Sep 1880/D at the res of her husband near Concord Fri 3 Sep of typhoid fever, Mrs. J. R. Manship, age 63 yrs.

D at Wye Landing Talb Co 5 Sep of dysentery, James Holmes only s/o Emory R. and Annie K. Burnite, age 4 yrs.

DJ 18 Sep 1880/M Tues morning 14 Sep at the res of the bride's parents near Henderson by Rev W. P. Davis of Dover, Fred Burgess of Dover and Miss Virgie Culbreth.

D at the res of her parents 28 Aug Etta d/o Author and Mary E. Webber, age 4 yrs and 6 weeks.

DJ 25 Sep 1880/M at the res of the groom's parents Thurs last by Rev James Rich, George Price and Miss Sallie Downes, both of this county.

M at Union Grove parsonage 21 Sep by Rev W. J. D. Lucas, Mr. W. K. Murphy and Miss H. J. Andrew, all of Caroline Co.

D at his res in Tuckahoe Neck Mon evening last, after a short illness of gastric fever, Thomas H. Ford, in the 36th yr.

D in Denton Thurs evening last, Phenor, d/o Rebecca and Alexander Griffin, age about 5 yrs.

D at his res near Potters Landing Mon last, Christian Richmond, age about 70 yrs.

DJ 2 Oct 1880/D near Denton Sun morning last after a long illness, Mrs. Sarah Wilson wife of Joshua Wilson.

DJ 9 Oct 1880/D in Bethlehem 1st inst, Mrs. Davis in the 81st yr.

D 24 Sep, Sallie Wilson, age 50 yrs.

DJ 16 Oct 1880/William Conaway, a carpenter of Lewes, jumped from a scaffold about two weeks ago and by so doing ran a nail into his foot which caused lock-jaw and resulted in his death on Tues last.

DJ 23 Oct 1880/James Pippin, age 98 yrs, of QA Co, d at his res near Bridgetown last Sat. He was blind and helpless for several yrs past. He served in the War of 1812. He spent most of his life in that county.

Sat afternoon last William Dewing s/o Rev T. S. Dewing who res 4 miles from Centreville in Spaniard's Neck was shot in the stomach in a hunting accident. (Long item)

D in this town Thurs, Mrs. Lucretia Bishop, about 84 yrs old.

DJ 30 Oct 1880/M at the M.E. Parsonage Greensborough on the evening of 20th inst by Rev J. E. Smith, Robert H. Christopher and Miss Mary Pritchett, both of this county.

M at the res of Edward Saulsbury near Denton 20 Oct by Rev Dr. J. F. Boone, John R. Boone and Miss Kate Collison, all of this county.

M 20th inst at the res of the bride's parents near Burrsville by Rev J. M. Elderdice, John T. Smith to Miss Eunice J. Blades, both of Kent Co Md.

M 27th inst at the M.P. Parsonage at Burrsville by Rev J. M. Elderdice, Robert D. Clark to Miss Sarah E. Stokeley, both of this county.

D Thurs 14 Oct near Roseville, Mrs. Rebecca Faulkner, age about 65 yrs.

D in Greensborough Sat morning 16th inst, Herbert s/o William Minner age 4 yrs.

D at Bridgetown 14th inst, infant s/o William and Mary Graham.

DJ 6 Nov 1880/M at Union Grove Parsonage 28 Oct by Rev W. J. Lucas, John Covey and Miss Emma J. Smith.

D at his res near Smithville Thurs 17 Oct of Bright's disease, H(?) J. Pennypacker.

D in Oxford 8 Oct, Samuel Sparklin, age 68 yrs.

D at his res near Henderson Tues last, Richard Ross, age about 75 yrs.

DJ 13 Nov 1880/M at the res of the bride 3 Nov, Henry C. Booker to Miss Cora E. Morris, all of this county.

M 3rd inst at M.E. Church at East New Market by Rev R. W. Todd, Rev Wilber F. Corkran of Wilmington Conference and Miss Josephine Fleming of East New Market, Dorch Co.

M in New York City Wed 27 Oct by Rev Dr. Beyan, Edwin M. Wood of "Rosebut Lodge," Dorch Co, and Mrs. Annie Crawford of New York City.

M Tues morning last by Rev S. D. Hall(?), Rector of the Episcopal Church in this place, Mr. Z. P. Steele of the Caroline Democrat and Miss Sallie P. Reynor, both of this town.

M Tues evening last at M. E. Church by Rev A. W. Milby, Francis A. Redden and Miss Emma Stewart, all of this place.

D at Spring Grove Hospital Balt Co on 3rd inst of paralysis, Peter B. Pritchett, late of this town in the 76th yr.

D at his res near Burrsville Mon last, Lewis Ward formerly of Del, about 65 yrs.

D 30 Oct last, Rachel F. wife of James Corkran, age 51 yrs.

D at his res near Bethlehem Fri 25 Oct, Capt John P. Todd, age 50 yrs.

DJ 30 Nov 1880/On Thrus the 1st during the temporary absence to a distant part of the farm a 7-year old daughter of Mr. and Mrs. John Lare res near Bloomery, this county, poured coal oil on the fire when the can exploded, burning the child so severely that she died in a few hours.

M Tues 9 Nov at the res of Henry Dager near Dover by Rev C. Huntington, Walter Booker of Hillsborough to Miss Amanda Broadway of Willow Grove Del.

M at the res of the bride's father 10 Nov by Rev J. Mowbray, Mr. O. P. Mowbray of Phila formerly of this county and Miss Tina Calloway of Harrington Del.

M Tues 9 Nov at Christ Church Balt by Rev W. F. Watkins, Clinton W. Phillips of Pittsburg and Carrie N. D/o Thomas N. Gould of Balt.

M Luther T. Williams and Miss Emma Pierce, both of QA Co.

Newspaper Abstracts

D near town Thurs night last of diphtheria, Lawrence 4th s/o Charles A. and Ella Dunning, age 4 yrs, 5 mos, 18 das.

D at Federalsburg Mon 8 Nov of consumption, Mrs. Celia Wright, in the 61st yr.

DJ 27 Nov 1880/Sara Cephas colored wife of Uriah Cephas res near Harmony d very suddenly Mon night last. She had been engaged all day in daily labor, but was taken at 3 o'clock with paralysis and d about 11 o'clock the same night. She was about 60 yrs old.

Col. James E. Douglas d at this res in Preston Mon last. He was attacked a few days before his death with a severe form of typhoid pneumonia. He was born in Dorch Co in 1820. From early life to 1847 he was a carpenter. He m Mary C. d/o James Davis, his mother's cousin to whom he had been given in childhood. He removed to Caroline Co near Preston in 1854. In 1866 his wife d leaving him four children - all sons. He m the following year Mrs. Ann Elizabeth Clarke d/o Joseph Mowbray. (More information on his career)

M at the res of Dr. G. M. Fisher in the town Thurs 25 Nov by Rev James H. Rich, John W. Gootee and Miss Josephine Brannen.

M at Sheppard Chapel Thurs 25th inst by Rev J. E. Smith, Charles H. Blackiston and Miss Laura Roe.

M at Wesley Chapel Tues evening 16th inst by Rev J. E. Smith, Charles Baynard and Miss Laura Layton.

D in Bridgetown 3 Nov of diphtheria, the only d/o William and Elizabeth Straughn, 3 yrs and 3 mos old.

DJ 4 Dec 1880/M 24th ult in Harrington by Rev England, George F. Noble of Caroline Co and Miss Martha A. Wroten of Kent Co Del.

DJ 11 Dec 1880/D of diptheria Mon 6th inst, Araminta May d/o Daniel and Annie Gibbons, age 7 yrs and 4 mos.

Mr. Charles Lake, Clerk of the Dorch Co Court, his wife, and eight children, have been afflicted with a malignant fever. Son Willie age 19 yrs d Thurs week last. The others are convalescent.

AU 16 Dec 1880/Robert Jarrel d Sun evening last who was for many yrs one of the associate Judges of the Orphans Court of this county, about 60 yrs of age, afflicted with a tumor in the stomach. (Long item)

D at her res near Preston Tues 30 Nov of gastroenteritis, Nancy wife of Henry Dean, age 73 yrs.

DJ 18 Dec 1880/D 13th inst of bronchial consumption, Poulson E. Hubbard, age 52 yrs and 6 mos. He d near his home near Union Grove Mon afternoonlast. Mr. Hubbard spent his whole life in this county. He leaves a wife and children.

M at the res of William Tharp near Vernon by Rev A. W. Milby, Henry T. Nuttle of Anderstontown and Emma Hopkins of Vernon.

AU 23 Dec 1880/James T. Conner d at Cambridge last Fri night who for many yrs was clerk on the Highland Light of the Maryland Steamboart Company but resigned about two yrs ago to engage as a traveling salesman for Hurst, Miller and Co of Balt.

M at Bloomery Church Thurs evening 9 Dec by Rev Fisher, William Robinson and Miss Elizabeth E. Liden, all of this county.

M in this town 9 Dec by Rev A. W. Milby, Joshua Porter and Sarah F. Buckmaster.

Newspaper Abstracts

M 15th inst at Thawley's Chapel by Rev John E. Smith, Howard Griffith to Miss Ida Lord.

A tribute to the memory of Lettie Todd, signed Mollie.

AU 30 Dec 1880/The story is going the rounds about the case of Godfrey Parnett a Hungarian who settled in the county serveral yrs ago and who two yrs since was bereft of reason and sent to the Maryland Insane Hospital but returned home but is still a raging maniac.

William Wilkinson until a few yrs ago a citizen of this county d at his res in Balt Co 9th inst having resided in Tuckahoe Neck the greater portion of his life.

M 24th inst by Rev R. W. Todd P.E. of Dover Dist, Rev J. M. Lindale of the Wilmington Annual Conference and Miss Annie Thawley.

M 22nd inst by Rev J. E. Smith, George L. Griffith and Miss Georgie E. Bartlett, all of this county.

D near Fowling Creek 13 Dec of diptheria, Anna Violett d/o F. S. and Elizabeth Todd, age 2 yrs, 5 mos, 19 das.

DJ 25 Dec 1880/107 marriage licenses have been issued in 1880 to date of which 27 were colored. In 1879 82 had been issued and in 1878 88 had been issued.

Abstracts from Easton Newspapers
Republican Star and General Advertiser

19 Oct 1813/M Tues last by Rev Sharpley, Rev John Emory of QA Co to Miss Caroline Sellers of Caroline Co.

8 Sep 1829/M Wed evening last by Rev George G. Cookman, Samuel Meloney of Hillsborough to Miss Mary M. Clifton of Talb Co.

D in Caroline Co Fri 14th ult, Mrs. Mahala consort of John Jump, after a long and tedious illness, in the 37 yr. She was a member of the Meth Church for about 15 yrs. She left a husband and 7 children.

Easton Gazette 30 Jul 1831

M Tues evening last by Rev Thomas Bayne, Dr. A. M. White of Greensborough, s/o Rev Alward White to Miss Margaret Elizabeth only d/o Rev Lott Warfield of this town (Easton).

D in Caroline Co on Thurs last, Rebecca E. d/o Daniel Chezum, age 9 yrs and 12 das.

AU 30 OCT 1860 - M 18 OCT by Rev E. Miller, Joseph Guest to Elizabeth Barwick, all of Centreville.

AU 30 MAY 1867 - M 23 May at the res of the bride's parents by Rev. John Ault, Dr. H. Clay Kemp of Denton & Mollie E. Zacharias of Mechanisburg, PA.

AU 15 Jun 1871 - Charles Willis d at Federalsburg on Sunday 11 Jun from a cancer, age about 73

AU 14 Jun 1877 - M at the res of C. E. Jarrell 3 Jun by Rev George T. Tyler, Mr. H. L. Gearhart formerly of PA to Mollie M. Cox formerly of Queen Anne's Co.

PART TWO

Mortality Schedules of 1850, 1860, 1870, and 1880

Information is given in the following sequence: name/age/sex/color/free or slave/married or widowed/month of death/occupation/cause of death/number of days of illness. In the 1870 schedule the election district is given. In the 1880 schedule the first number is family unit number given in the primary census schedule (schedule 1) of 1880. Additional information included at the end of the entry is place of birth of deceased, father, and mother; number of years as res of the county; place where disease was contracted if other than place of death; and attending physician. If color is white or place of birth is Maryland it is omitted.

Although each of these schedules is supposed to cover the period 1 June of the previous year to 1 June of the census year, one should not assume each death listed actually fell within this period. For instance, the 1869-1870 listing shows the death of M. C. Emerson as June. One would expect the death to have occurred in June 1869; however, the death actually occurred on June 24, 1870 as revealed in the 30 June 1870 issue of the American Union.

1850 Mortality Schedule

1. Rich, William 6 mos male Black free Nov
2. Suprry, Mary 4 mos female Aug
3. Spurry, Sarah 2 mos female Aug
4. Bishop, Mary 30 female married Mar/consumption
5. Canady, Jane 7 mos female Black free Oct
6. Green, Henrietta 21 female Black free Mar
7. Cooper, Rhody 71 female Black free married Oct/Old age
8. Milby, George 1 male Sep/billious fever/3 day sickness
9. Roe, Frances 11 male Aug
10. Last name not given, Gibbs 14 male Black slave
11. Last name not given, Sarah 3 female Black slave
12. Last name not given, Jane 1 mo female Black slave
13. Thawley, William 69 male married farmer/disease of the heart/sudden
14. Baggs, Sarah E. 5 female Sep
15. Straughan, William E. 29 male Mar farmer/tyfoid fever/3 das
16. Thomas, Margaret A. 37 female Aug/consumption/4 week sickness
17. Manering, Joseph 45 male married Aug/disentary/2 das
18. Last name not given, Ann 27 female Black free Mar/Sudden
19. Manering, Jane 37 female Aug/disentary
20. Thomas, Sewell 1 male Black free Jun
21. Matthews, Ann 2 female Black free Mar/sudden
22. Morgan, Mary E. 22 female married Mar/plurisey/3 das
23. Whitby, John 35 male Dec/A(ff?) throat/4 das
24. Scribner, Mary 8 mos female Black free Mar/b(urn)
25. Wheeler, Rebecca 75 female married Oct/Old age
26. Causey, Lo(urise)y 22 female Black free Feb
27. Thomas Albert 25 male Black free Mar labourer
28. Satterfield, James 60 male widowed May
29. Hicks, John 80 male Black free Mar Labourer/Old age
30. Rathele, Mary 39 female married Feb
31. Cooper, James 42 male married Nov carpenter/A(recipad)ous
32. James, Ann 80 female widowed Jun/Old age
33. Harriss, James 1 mo Oct

34. Tharp, Margaret 53 female widowed Jul/3 das
35. Matthews, Mary 83 female widowed Jul/cholera/4 das
36. Roe, Thomas 63 male married Apr farmer/consumption
37. Pearson, Joseph 2 mos male Sep/cause of death unknown
38. Corkran, Willis 5 male Jul/dyerea
39. Harriss, David 1 male Aug/dysentary/3 das
40. Smith, Elizabeth 1 mo female Black free Dec/cause of death unknown
41. Garretson, Sarah 40 female married Jan/cause of death unknown/4 das
42. Turner, Thomas 26 male Oct merchant/cause of death unknown/4 das
43. Turner Pr(ue)ll(a) 31 female Mar/consumption
44. Daviss, Mary 1 mo female Jan
45. Faulkner, Julia A. 8 mos female Jul/injured brain
46. Hudson, William H. 8 male Feb/croup/sudden
47. Saulsbury 38 male married May farmer/sudden
48. Parris, John born in Del, 40 male married Jun farmer/cause of death unknown
49. Andrew, John W. 21 male May labourer/sudden
50. Scott, Harrison 4 male Black free Apr
51. Christopher, Loucinda 35 female married Mar/consumption/12 das
52. Atwell, Benjamin 86 male widower May/dysentary
53. Taylor, Jacob 60 male Black free married Feb sailor/consumption/20 das
54. Wright, Peter 46 male married Sep farmer/dropsy
55. Smith, John 47 male married May farmer/plurisey
56. Nicols, Meranda 6 mos female Sep/cause of death unknown
57. Willis, Thomas 18 male May labourer/tyfoid fever/6 das
58. Eaton 6 mos female Jul/dysentary/10 das
59. Chaffinch, Jane 20 female married Apr/billious/12 das
60. Kenton, Margritt 67 female married May/dropsy/10 das
61. Chrisman, Elizabeth 29 female married May/consumption/2 mos
62. Harriss, James 23 male Black free Sep labourer/billious/5 das
63. (S)lawford, Susan 90 female Black free Jun/Old age
64. Rickets, Mary 45 female Apr
65. Murry, Isadore 5 female Feb
66. Collins, Deborah 1 mo female Jan
67. Stewart, Ann M. 22 female married Dec-Confinement/4 das
68. Last name not given, John 2 mos male Black slave
69. Willoughby, Elizabeth 68 female widowed Dec/Consumption
70. Nicolson, Alexander 2 male Dec/Injured brain/3 das
71. Coey, Eliza 40 female Nov/Dis of the liver
72. Covey, Mary 26 female married Sep/kicked by horse
73. Stevins, Samuel 31 male Feb labourer/Consumption
74. Lister, Elizabeth A. 2 female Sep/Dysentary
75. Hicks, James 21 male Apr labourer/Pluricy/6 das
76. Last name not given, Perry 3 male Black slave July/Sudden

Remarks: The water is fresh and good, the land is of different soils
mostly sandy and level. White oak, black oak, hickory and pine timber
are the predominent growth of wood. Marl abounds in large quantities
in some sections of the country.

1860 Mortality Schedule

1. Flowers, James H. 6 male Oct/dropsey/20 das
2. White, Elizabeth 75 female widowed Sep/unknown cause of death/6 das
3. Connelly, Sallie 2 mos female Mar-Unknown/5 das
4. Burton, Elizabeth 46 female married Dec-Liver disease/60 das
5. Hicks, Robert 12 male Black slave Sep-Dropsy/50 das
6. Chairs, William 1 male Black slave Feb-Unknown 5 das
7. Gullet, Parrent T. 1 male Sep-Whooping Cough/30 das
8. Hall, Elizabeth 7 mos female Aug-Summer complaint/20 das
9. Green, William 22 male Sep farm hand-Bilious fever/21 das
10. Gibson, Samuel 1 mos male Black slave Oct-Overlaid/1 day
11. Wilson, Marriah 33 female married Dec-Consumption/150 das
12. Simpson, John 5 mos male Aug-Summer complaint/30 das
13. Wayman, Benjamin 37 male Black free married Sep farmhand-Tyfoid Fever/6 das
14. Warner, Sarah 4 mos female Black free Nov-Unknown/Sudden
15. Orrell, Ida 6 mos female May-Unknown/2 weeks
16. Ash, Sarah 24 female Black free married Oct-Consumption/3 mos
17. G(i)ver, Elijah 21 male Black free farm hand-Liver disease/2 weeks
18. Jewell, Charles H. 2 male Aug-Unknown/1 month
19. Rouse, Mary 40 female Apr-Liver disease/1 month
20. Graham, John 36 male married Mar merchant-Liver disease/1 month
21. Roe, Sarah A. 51 female widowed May-Heart disease/3 mos
22. Wilkinson, Etholinda 30 female Black free widowed Feb-Consumption/5 mos
23. Sephus, Gertrude 2 female Black slave May-Summer disease/3 wks
24. Black, Alla 2 mos female Black slave May-Summer disease/10 das
25. Garner, Alexine 15 female Aug-Nervous fever/1 month
26. Dill, John T. 2 male May-Summer disease/3 wks
27. Rust, Jeremiah 78 male married May farmer-Consumption/4 years
28. Grove, Levina (5) mos female Mulatto free Sep-Thrush/2 mos
29. Hardcastle, Annie 6 mos female June-Summer disease/2 das
30. Downs, Cla(ir) 6 mos female Aug-Whooping Cough/1 month
31. Hodges, Martha 20 female Black free married Feb-Unknown/ 3 wks
32. Watson, Sarah 55 female Black free married Apr-Dropsy/3 wks
33. Hubbard, James 63 male married Sep carpenter-Consumption/6 mos
34. Towers, James H. 27 male married Apr farmer-Tyfoid fever/2 mos
35. Prattes, John 1 month male Black free Apr-Unknown/1 week
36. Perry, Margaret 45 female married Dec-Consumption/4 mos
37. Haines, Irena 30 female Black free widowed Dec-Consumption/5 mos
38. Benden, Robert 8 mos Feb-Unknown/(?)
39. Tilghman, Daniel 67 male Black free married Dec farm hand-Unknonwn/Sudden

1870 Mortality Schedule

1. Scribner, (Air)y 9 mos female Black May/consumption/2nd dist
2. Norriss, Richard 73 male Apr farmer/dropsy/1st dist
3. Carlisle, Charles 1 mo male Sep/croup/1st dist
4. Clarke, Sallie 2 female Delware Jul/whooping cough/1st dist
5. Shearwood, Margaret 50 female Jul/consumption/1st dist
6. Lewis, Clinton 2 male Nov/tyfoid/1st dist
7. Downes, Benjamin A. 14 male Jan/accidently shot himself/1st dist
8. Meredith, Lavisa 76 female married Apr keeping house/apoplexy/1st dist
9. Berry, Henrietta 52female Black married May keeping house/consumption/2nd dist
10. Wilkerson, Robert J. 8 male Black Sep/paralysis/2nd dist
11. Gibson, Robert H. 25 male Aug clerk in store/dropsy/2nd dist

12. Laws, Sammuel H. 7 mos male Dec/brain fever/1st dist
13. Straughn, Thomas Rev 78 male married Oct local minister/paralysis/1st dist
14. Miller, Sarah M. 32 female Nov/consumption/1st dist
15. Bantum, Adaline 45 female Black married Mar/consumption/1st dist
16. Bell, Maggie 10 mos female Oct/measles/2nd dist
17. Green Eliza 40 female Black married Aug/congestion of liver/2nd dist
18. McMannis, James 5 male May/pneumonia/2nd dist
19. Russum, Rhoda 38 female married Jan/pneumonia/2nd dist
20. Outen, James Fletcher 3 mos male Delaware Mar/whooping cough/2nd dist
21. Carnery, Henrietta 21 female Black married Sep/consumption/2nd dist
22. Kenney, Bartie 22 female married Dec/mania/2nd dist
23. Slaughter, Isabel 3 female Delaware Jan/whooping cough/2nd dist
24. Swann, Mary 45 female Dec/consumption/2nd dist
25. Swann, Henrietta 14 female Jul/dysentery/2nd dist
26. Pearson, Miss Kate 26 female Dec/consumption/2nd dist
27. Draper, Margaret A. 34 female married Feb 16/pneumonia/3rd dist
28. Connelly, Airy A. 28 female married Dec/child birth/3rd dist
29. Brown, Edward Constantine 30 male Dec Captain/consumption 3rd dist
30. Gadd, Mary E. 34 female married Aug/consumption/3rd dist
31. Turner, Laura Euphema 1 female Aug/infant cholera/3rd dist
32. McFarlane, Charlotte S. 33 female married England Mar/tyfoid/3rd dist
33. Mansfield, Mary V. 9 mos female Jul/croup/3rd dist/whooping cough
34. Letty, Laura A.(?) 15 female Mar/congestive liver/3rd dist
35. Wilson, Florence 9 mos female Jul/croup/3rd dist
36. Ridgley, Francis Piercy 1 male Feb/whooping cough/3rd dist
37. Williams, Susan Effa 1 female Feb/pneumonia/3rd dist
38. Emerson, Elizabeth R. 1 female New Jersey Oct/cholera infanta/Denton
39. Emerson, Marion Clinton 7 mos New Jersey Jun/cholera infanta/Denton
40. Sownes, Raymond W. 8 mos male Sep/cholera infanta/Denton
41. Truxon, James 6 mos male Black Jan/whooping cough/Denton
42. Smith, Mary Florence 2 female Jul/whooping cough/Denton
43. Smith, Henry H. 42 male married Aug/tree fell on him/Denton
44. Blockson, David 42 male Delaware married Aug atty at law/inflamation of the bowels/3rd dist
45. Williams, William A. 35 male married Jan farmer/consumption/3rd dist
46. Hough, Walter 36 male married Feb farmer/pneumonia/3rd dist
47. Ellwanger, Hartley 34 male Pennsylvania married Oct farmer/intermittent billious fever/3rd dist
48. Ross, Enoch 45 male Black married Jan farmer/pneumonia 3rd dist
49. Grinage, Solomon 66 male married Apr farmer/apoplexy/3rd dist
50. Davis, John 40 male Black married May labourer/pneumonia/3rd dist
51. Alpheus, Susan 45 female Black married Apr/pneumonia and billious fever/3rd dist
52. Webster, Thomas 72 male Delaware married Mar farmer/consumption/3rd dist
53. Peper, Robert 50 male Delaware married Mar farmer/plurisy/3rd dist
54. Bell, George 60 male Black married Dec farmer/disease of the heart/3rd dist
55. Wyatt, Louisa 33 female married Jun/consumption/3rd dist
56. Emerson, Sarah L. 50 female married Mar/consumption/3rd dist Denton
57. Towns, George E. 20 male New Hampshire Jul/epileptic fits/3rd dist
58. Evetts, Ann 70 female May/unknown cause of death/3rd dist
59. Jopp, Edward 3 mos male foreign parents Jul/cholera infantum/3rd dist
60. Wood, Martha 15 female Apr/pneumonia/3rd dist
61. Lang, Samuel 60 male married Dec farmer/consumption/3rd dist

1870 Mortality Schedule

62. Kemp, John W. 9 mos male Mar/whooping cough/3rd dist
63. Hubbard, Mary 95 female married Mar keeping house/asthma/3rd dist
64. Wootters, Laurzey 40 female married Aug keeping house/billious fever/ 3rd dist
65. Trice, Laura 2 female Feb/whooping cough/3rd dist
66. Miller, Martha 7 mos female Feb/whooping cough
67. Griffith, Ann W. S. 50 female married Jun/consumption/3rd dist
68. Argo, Charles 5 mos male Jul/cholera infantum/3rd dist
69. Simpson, Thompson T. 45 male married Jan tailor/consumption/3rd dist
70. Collins, Abram Y. 57 male married Sep farmer/tyfoid fever/4th dist
71. Willis, Henry(?) male Nov farmer/consumption/4th dist
72. Deen, Lacy 1 male Aug/cholera infantum/4th dist
73. Wentworth, Ester 15 female Maine Oct/tyfoid fever/4th dist
74. Friend, James 75 male Black married Sep farmer/consumption/4th dist
75. Be(w)ly, Mary 30 female Black married Jun keeping house/consumption/4th dist
76. Causey, Henrietta 9 mos female Black Jul/measles/4th dist
77. Rich, Charles W. 3 mos male Black May/unknown cause of death/4th dist
78. Wheeler, Henrietta V. 5 mos female Feb farmer/whooping cough/4th dist
79. Friend, Gabriel 80 male Black married Jun/tyfoid fever/4th dist
80. Fluharty, William 38 male married Apr sailor/pneumonia/4th dist
81. Coulbourn, Alverde 4 mos female May/cholera infantum/4th dist
82. Sharp, Margaret 38 female Black married Mar keeping house/consumption/4th dist
83. Stevens, Wilbert W. 2 mos male Jun/cholera infantum/4th dist
84. Stevens, Martha L. 3 mos female Jul/cholera infantum/4th dist
85. Parker, John 55 male Jun labourer/scrofula/4th dist
86. James, Anna C. 17 female Black Jul domestic servant/pneumonia/5th dist
87. Jester, Peter 68 male married Mar farmer/pneumonia/5th dist
88. Nichols, Henry 1 mo male mar/unknown cause of death
89. Wilson, John 2 male Pennsylvania Jan/cerbro spinal meningitis/5th dist
90. Wilson, Anna 6 female Pennsylvania May/inflamation of the heart/5th dist
91. Connelly, Rebecca 84 female married Oct/neuralgia/5th dist
92. Barnes, George R. 1 mo male May/unknown cause of death
93. Connelly, Britana 68 female married Aug keeping house/cancer
94. Sullivan Jacob 15 male Feb farm laborer/diabetes/5th dist
95. Andrew, Charles 45 male married May carpenter/consumption 5th dist
96. Sedgwick, Sarah A. 3 female Delaware Jun/dysentery/5th dist
97. Sheppard, Adam 85 male Black married Jan/pneumonia/5th dist
98. Cook, Clara 6 mos female Black Feb/whooping cough/5th dist
99. Bowdle, Daniel 50 male married Apr laborer/consumption/5th dist
100. Ricketts, James 3 mos Black Apr/unknown cause of death/5th dist
101. Cannon, Jane 12 female Black Sep/tyfoid fever 5th dist

1880 Mortality Schedule

1st District

Number of family unit as listed in primary schedule, schedule 1/name/age/sex/
race if other than white/married or single/state of birth of deceased, father,
mother/occupation/month of death/cause of death/number of years residing in
Caroline Co/place disease was contracted if other than place of death/attending
physician

112 Booker, Robert/72/male/married/Md, Md, Md/wheelwright/Apr/paralysis/11/
Alex Hardcastle
67 Bradshaw, James W(?)/13/male/Black/single/Md, Md, Md/farm laborer/Sep/diptheria/
13/QA Co/J. B. Zook(?)
74 Connelly, Henry/68/male/white/single/Md, Md, Md/farmer/Apr/paralysis/27/
James R. Wilson(?)

86   Vane/9 das/female/single/Md, Md, Md/Mar/pneumonia/No attending physician
87   Done, Babeck S./2 mos/male/Del, N.J., Del/Jul/pneumonia/contracted in Del/
J. V. Knotts/death occurred in Kent Co Del
92   Tumy R. H./2/male/Black/single/Md, Md, Md/Jul/dysentery/J. V. Knotts
95   Jones, Wesley/55(?)/male/Black/male/Md, Md, Md/farmer laborer/Aug/Diarrhea/
17 mos in the county/no attending physician

99   Bridles, Rebecca/67(?)/female/widow/Md, Md, Md/Apr/unknown cause of death/
no attending physician
97   Kilson/1 mo/male/Black/single/Md, Md, Md/Jul/dysentery/no attending physician
111 Potts, Adaline/1/female/Black/single/Md, Md, Md/Sep/croup/J. V. Knotts
119 Wilkerson, Emma/16/female/Black/Md, Md, Md/d at home/consumption, hemmorhage
from the lungs/Dr. Evans (Apr)
137 Long, William/10/male/Del, Pa, Del/d at home/Feb/pneumonia/S. B. Thomas
149 McCullough, William/12/male/single/Md, Md, - /d at home/Feb/diptheria/11 yrs
in the county/S. B. Thomas
149 McCullough, Fred/5/male/single/Md, Md, -/d at home/Mar/diptheria/5 mos in
the county/S. B. Thomas
149 McCullough, Anna/3/female/single/Md, Md, -/d at home/Mar/diptheria/3 yrs in
the county/McClyments
174 Mathias Thias/74/male/Black/married/Md, Md, Md/farmer laborer/Dec/diptheria,
74 yrs in the county/no attending physician
179 Chiffins(?), Elizabeth/74/female/widow/Del, Del, Del/Nov/paralysis/4 yrs in
the county/Alex Hardcastle
187 Jones S. M./48/female/single/Md, Md, Md/farming/Aug/paralysis/George W.
Goldsboro
215 Henry Frank/43/male/Black/married/Md, Md, Md/farm   laborer/Mar/consumption/
Alex Hardcastle
228 Kirk, William G./13/male/single/Del, Del, Del/farm laborer/Feb/accidentally
shot/11 yrs in the county/S. B. Thomas
270 Downs, John W./17/male/single/Md, Md, Md/farm laborer/Dec/typhoid fever/17
yrs in the county/Dr. Graham
298 Hackett, William/39(?)/male/Black/married/Md, Md, Md/farm laborer/Mar/result
of an accident/39 yrs in the county/accident occurred in Del/William F. Davis
299 Bradshaw, Martha/22(?)/female/Black/married/Md, Md, Md/keeping house/Nov/
hemmorhage from the lungs/22 yrs in the county/G. W. Parvis
155 Pritchet, Winfred/7 mos/male/Md, Md, Md/d at home/Aug/cholera infantum/
S. B. Thomas
156 Dunnelly, F. Olin/53/male/white(?)/male/N.C., N.C., N.C./physician/Dec/
congestion of the brain/S. B. Thomas
284 Sudler, Mary E./32(?)/female/Black/married/Md, Md, Md/keeping house/Oct/
consumption/8 yrs in the county/Dr. Graham
285 Thomas, Mary/70(?)/female/Black/Md, Md, Md/Dec/dropsy/no attending physician
... Tribet, Anne/57/female/married/Ga, Ga, Ga/carpet weaver/Oct/pneumonia/Thomas

Addition to Greensboro from physicians' registers:
     Spencer, William H./4/male/single/Md, Md, Md/Mar/burned/Betson
     Cole, Fanny C./4 mos/female/single/Md, Md, Md/Mar/unknown cause of death/
Judson
     Smith, Ethel/-/female/single/Md, Md, Md/Mar/still born/Judson
     Mason, child/0/male/Black/Md, Md, Md/Apr/still born/Judson
     Smith, Sarah/19/female/single/Md, Md, Md/servant/May/chronic pneumonia/
Betson
     Griffith, child/3 mos/male/single/Md, Md, Md/Nov/croup/Betson
     Croplers(?), Elijah/54/male/married/Md, Md, Md/shoemaker/Oct/heart disease/
Betson

1880 Mortality Schedule

2nd District - Greensboro District

6   Massey, Florence/4/female/single/Md, Md, Md/Feb/membranous croup/4 yrs in the county/Dr. H. C. Comegys
2   Case, Eliza/65/female/married/Md, Md, Md/keeping house/Oct/unknown inflamation/Comegys
15 Bonn(?), Richard/72/male/widower/Md, Prussia, Md/Tobacconist/M../Rheumatic(?)/G. W. Goldsboro
19 Rhodes, John E./1/male/single/Md, Pa; Del/Oct/croup/1 yr in the county/H. C. Comegys
25 Carroll, Nettie/7/female/married/Md, Md, Md/Oct/diptheria/7 yrs in the county/H. C. Comegys
27 Stayton, Orville T./4/male/Md, Del, Del/Apr/drowned/4 yrs in the county/H. C. Comegys
29 Birmingham, Mary/1/female/single/Md, Md, Md/Aug/dysentery/1 yr in the county/Dr. Hocking/death occurred in Easton, Talb Co
42 Cooper/2 mos/female/Black/single/Md, Md, Md/Feb/congestion of the lungs/H. C. Comegys
58 Horsey, Turpin/5/male/single/Md, Del, Va/Nov/croup/4 yrs in the county/Comegys
59 Sipple, James L./2 mos/male/single/Md, Del, Md/Apr/unknown cause/Comegys
64 Gray, Miriam/29/female/married/Md, Del, Del/keeping house/Jul/consumption/29 yrs in the county/Betson
83 Lock, Julia E./3 mos/female/Black/single/Md, Md, Md/Aug/catarh(?)/3 mos in the county/Betson
90 Dobbs, Lillian A./2/female/single/Md, N.Y., N.Y./May/consumption/2 yrs in the county/Comegys
113 Dabson, Edward/60/male/married/Md, Md, Md/farmer/Sep/consumption/60 yrs in the county/Comegys
130 Blades, William J./9 das   /male/single/Md, Md, Md/Apr/cholera infantum/Betson
159 Weaver, Hattie S./10 mos/female/single/Md, Pa, Pa/Aug/summer complaint/Comegys
177 Hobbs, Benjamin/1/male/single/Md, Md, Md/Sep/slow fever(orchard fever?)/1 yr in the county/Goldsboro
183 Downs, William/3/male/Black/single/Md, Md, Md/Feb/unknown cause/3 yrs in the county
186 Brown, Mary J./15/female/Black/single/15 yrs in the county/Goldsboro Md, Md, Md/unemployed/Dec/Pneumonia
223 Lockerman/1 mo/male/Black/single/Md, Md, Md/Mar/unknown cause/1 mo in the county
236 Baggs, Thomas/62/male/married/England, England, England/unemployed/Nov/heart disease/3 yrs in the county/Hardcastle
237 Cox, William 60/male/married/Md, Md, Md/farmer/May/inflamation/1 yr in the county/Warner/death occurred in Kent Co Del
292 Waters(?), Ella C./2 mos/female/Black/Md, Md, Md/Sep/summer complaint
292 Clark, Francina/45/female/Black/single/Md, Md, Md/unemployed/Apr/spasisms/45 yrs in the county
300 Carroll/12 das)/male/Md, Del, Del/Dec/cholera infantum/Dr. Young
345 Pippin/2 mos/male/single/Md, Md, Md/Aug/cholera infantum/Comegys
345 Pippin, Bessie/3/female/single/Md, Md, Md/Apr/croup/3 yrs in the county/Comegys
346 Smith, Alexander/2/male/Black/single/Md, Md, Md/May croup/2 yrs in the county/Comegys
360 Morris(?), Mary C./26/female/single/Md, Md, Md/unemployed/Jun/typhoid fever/26 yrs in the county/Betson

409 Lewis, Isabelle/25/female/Black/married/Md, Md, Md/keeping house/Dec/
epulepsy/25 yrs in the county/Goldsboro
414 Cooper, Perry H./8/male/Black/Md, Md, Md/Jul/burned to death/8 yrs in the
county
422 Thomas, Noah A. C./5 male/white(?)/Md, Md, Md/Nov/worm fever/5 yrs in the
county/Betson
471(?) Campbell, Rosa/2/female/single/Md, Md, Del/Dec/Croup/2 yrs in the conty/
C. Dudley/death occurred in QA Co
475 Covey, Charles/1/male/Black/single/Md, Md, Md/Jan/scarlet fever/1 yr in the
county
483 Hubbard, Ennalls/74/male/married/Md, Md, Md/farmer/Oct/piles/74 yrs in the
county/Comegys
469(?) Boone, Serena(?)/75/female/married/Md, Md, Md/keeping house/Dec/dropsy/
75 yrs in the county/Goldsboro

3rd election District
18   Williams, infant/male/Black/single/Md, Va, Md/Dec/premature
19   Wheeler, infant/female/Black/single/Md, Md, Md/Aug/still birth
19   Wheeler, infant/female/Black/single/Md, Md, Md/Apr/still birth
27   Sheppard, Matilda/50/female/Black/single/Md, Md, Md/washerwoman/May/apoplexy
25   Graham, infant/female/Del, Del, Del/Sep/premature
29   Gibson, Benjamin F./3/male/Black/single/Md, Md, Md/May/brain fever/Dr.
William H. Downes
75   Fountain, James A./33/male/widower/Md, Md, Md/traveling salesman/May/
consumption/Dr. Enoch George
130 Medford, Margaret/30/female/married/Del, Del, Del/keeping house/Jun/typhoid
fever/8 yrs in the county/Downes
136 Wallace, Rosa/6 female/single/Md, Pa, Md/Sep/gastric(?) fever/1 yr in the
county/Dr. George M. Fisher
136 Willoughby, infant/3 mos/female/single/Md, Md, Md/Jan/cranial abscess/3 mos
in the county/no attending physician
159 Passapae, James/67/male/married/Md, Md, Md/sailor/Oct/typhoid fever/19 yrs
in the county/George
185 Cranor, Angelina/30/female/married/Del, Del, Del/keeping house/Mar/
consumption/3 yrs in the county/Betson
183 Garrett, infant/1 mo/female/single/Md, Md, Md/Jun/Comegys
..6 Thomas, Georgia/3 mos/female/Black/single/Md, Md, Md/May/unknown cause/Dr.
Charles Williamson
205 Morgan, Sallie/28(or 29?)/female/single/Md, Md, Md/servant/Jan/consumption/
Williamson
.31 Thawley,   /died before this census year/Dr. J. W. Hignutt
234 Stokes, Mina E./1/female/single/Md, Md, Md/Aug/cholera, infantum/George
248 Baker, Martha J./35/female/married/Del, Del, Del/keeping house/Aug/
confinement/Salisbury
248 Baker, Martha/5 mos/female/single/Md, Del, Del/Mar/pneumonia/Salisbury
271 Sharp, Richard/65/male/Black/married/Del, -, -/blacksmith/Oct/paralysis/
Downes
271 Decoursey, Hestor/66/female/Black/single/Md, Md, Md/Mar/amputation/1 year
in the county/Downes
271 Willis, Margaret/80/female/Black/single/Md, Md, Md/Mar/old age/1 year in the
county/Downes
271 Covey, Martha/20/female/Md, Md, Md/Mar/dropsy/17 das/Downes
271 Hynson, Clarsy/50/female/Black/single/Md, -, -/Jun/dropsy/Downes
279 Porter, infant/male/single/Md, Md, Md/Aug/still birth/Williamson

1880 Mortality Schedule

280 Saulsbury, Corine/6 mos/female/single/Md, Md, Del/Jul/cholera infantum/
Fisher
331 Bullock, infant/1 day/male/single/Md, Del, Del/Mar/premature/Dr. Owings
349 Taylor, James M./2/male/single/Md, Md, Md/May/pneumonia/George
361 Brown, Julia E./38/female/single/Md, Md, Md/Apr/consumption/38 yrs in the
county/Williamson
386 Thawley, James/66/male/married/Del, -, -/farmer/Aug/consumption/14 yrs in
the county/Williamson
443 Thomas, Alexine/30/female/Black/single/Md, Md, Md/keeping house/Dec/
rheumatism/30 years in the county.
445 Cannon, Francis/30/male/single/Md, Md, Md/farming/Oct/congestion of the
brain/30 yrs in the county/Downes and George
446 Nuttle, Emma/15/female/single/Md, Md, Md/d at home/Apr/consumption/15 yrs
in the county/Hignutt
448 Purt, Annie/75/female/widow/Md, Md, Md/Jul/consumption/75/Hignutt
448 Purt, Charlie/2 days/male/single/Md, Md, Md/Sep/premature/Hignutt
451 Chance, Edward/4 mos/male/single/Md, Md, Md/Jun/dysentary
472 Driver, Joseph/77/male/Black/widower/Md, Md, Md/laborer/Dec/old age/Hignutt
516 Windsor, Emory J./9/male/single/Md, Md, Md/Jun/dropsy in brain/Dr. Hackett
523 Everngam, Thomas J./79/male/widower/Md, Md, Md/farmer/Feb/old age/Jefferson
529 Gravatt(?) __/1/female/single/Md, Pa, Md /laborer(sic)/Nov/cholora
infantum/Hignutt

Addition to third district from physician register:
    Haines, George W./49/male/Black/married/Md, Md, Md/farmer/Jun/dysentary/
Hignutt
    Dill, __/17/female/Md, Md, Md/Jan/Phithesis Pulin(?)/Saulsbury
    Dukes, Caroline/32/female/married/Md, Md, Md/housekeeper/Feb/liver disease
Judson

4th Election District
14 Beulah, Ann/84/female/Black/widow/Md, Md/Oct/unknown cause/35 yrs in
the county/no attending physician
31 Morgan, Eugene/12/male/single/Md, Del, Md/Sep/dysentery/3 yrs in the county/
Dawson
33 Infant/2 days/female/single/Md, Md, Md/Nov/unknown cause/no attending physician
44 Stanford, Ernest/3/male/Black/single/Md, Md, Md/Sep/brain disease/Hignutt
49 Chance, Thomas/31/male/single/Md, Md, Md/sailor/Oct/fracture of skull/31 yrs
in the county/hospital in Philadelphia
50 Infant/6 days/male/single/Md, Md, Md/Mar/unknown cause/Hignutt
97 Fletcher, Louiza/22/female/Black/married/Md, Md, Md/keeping house/consumption/
11 yrs in the county/Andrew Stafford
166 Payne, Noah Q./6 mos/male/single/Md, Md, Md/Aug/cutting teeth/Hignutt
169 Cheezum, John/68/male/married/Md, Md, Md/farmer/Sep/consumption/68/Hignutt
185 Williamson, Lacy E./6 months/male/single/Md, Md, Md/Jun/brain fever/Stafford
186 Andrew, Richard/72/male/single/Md, Md, Md/farmer/May/cancer/72 yrs in the
county/H. F. Willis
232 Murphy, James H./84/male/widower/Md, Md, Md/house carpenter/Sep/dysentery/
7 yrs in the county/Willis
238(?) Brown, Harriet/51/female/Black/married/Md, Md, Md/keeping house/Mar/
unknown cause/15 yrs in the county/Stafford
271(?) Towers, Sargent/35/female/married/Md, Md, Md/keeping house/Jun/childbirth/
35 yrs in the county/Stafford
... Lafayette/8 mos/female/Black/single/Md, Md, Md/May/cholera infantum
... Jenkins(?), Walter F./40/male/single/Md, Md, Md/Aug/typhoid fever/1 yr in
the county/Stafford

... ___, William J./3/male/single/Md, Md, Md/Aug/typhoid fever/1 yr in county/
Stafford
... Douglas, Mary C./3/female/single/Md, Md, Md/Jan/pneumonia/3 yrs in county/
Willis
337 Roe(?), Mary(?)/11/female/single/Md, Md, Md/Sep/consumption/3 yrs in the
county/Stafford
339(?) Perry(?), Sarah/67/female/widow/Del, Del, Del/keeping house/Apr/pneumonia
35 yrs in the county/Stafford
387(?) Jester Rebecca/59/female/married/Del, Del, Del/keeping house/Dec/
pneumonia/59 yrs in the county/Stafford
... Newcom(?), Mary F./20/female/Black/married/Md, Md, Md/keeping house/Nov/
consumption/20 yrs in the county/Willis
... Pool(?), Martha E./25/female/-/Md, Del, Md/keeping house/Sep/consumption/
25 yrs in the county/Stafford
... Webb(?), Amanda/14/female/Black/single/Md, Md, Md/Jul/scrofula/14 yrs in the
county/Stafford
.58(?) _____,___/1/male/Md, Md, Md/Aug/cholera infantum
.57 ___, Stephen(?) E./1/male/single/Md, Md, Md/Aug/cholera infantum
... Turner(?), Mary E./4/female/single/Md, Md, Md/Mar/pneumonia/4 months in the
county/Stafford
339(?) Jones, Charles W./3/male/single/Md, Md, Md,/May/meningitis/3 yrs in the
county/Stafford
... Hubbard, Jesse/69/male/married/Md, Md, Md/farmer/Jun/apoplexy/69 yrs in the
county/Willis
... Conaway, Elizabeth/32/female/married/Md, Md, Md/keeping house/Mar/burn/32 yrs.
in the county/Willis

Addition to fourth district from physician register:
    Brown(?), ___/67/female/Black/married/Md, Md, Md/May/cancer/Womb/Jefferson
    Neal(?), Martha/25/female/married/Md, Md, Md/farmers wife/Sep/consumption/
Jefferson
    Sharp, Annie/21/female/single/Md, Md, Md/Nov/consumption/Willis

5th District
20 Fields, Thomas/15/male/single/Md, N.Y.; Md/at school/Nov/addidently shot
himself in the woods/15 yrs in the county/Jefferson
24 Brumel, Samuel/3/male/Black/single/Md, Md, Md/Sep/croup/3 yrs in county
133 Wilson, John/50/male/married/Md, Md, Md/farmer/Jul/consumption/50 yrs in
the county/Jefferson
134 Trice, Sarah B./40(?)/female/single/Md, Md, Md/housekeeper/Jul/Menigitis/
20(?) yrs in the county/Meredith
... Butcher, Sophia/84/female/widow/N.J., -, -/Nov/typhiod fever/Meredith
126 Brumel, Amanda/2/female/Black/single/Md, Md, Md/Apr/catharah/2 yrs in the
county/Meredith
... Wright, Bascom/12/male/single/Md, Md, Md/at school/Nov/lock jaw/12 yrs in
the county/Jefferson
162 Sullivan, James C./1/male/single/Md, Md, Md/Aug/bilious dysentery
227(?) Covey(?), Emily/25/female/married/Del, Del, Del/house keeper/Feb/
consumption/Jefferson
... Camper, Roberta/4/female/Black/single/Md, Md, Md/Nov/chronic dysentary/4
yrs in the county/Jefferson
156 Dickerson, Joshua/34/male/Black/married/Md, Md, Md/laborer/Apr/obstruction
of bowels/34/Jefferson/died in Philadelphia
... Prattis, Lewis(?)/20/male/Black/single/Md, Md, Md/laborer/Feb/inflamation
of the bowels/2 yrs in the county/Jefferson

1880 Mortality Schedule

... Prattis, Edwin/3/male/Black/single/Md, Md, Md/Jan/pneumonia/3 yrs in the
county
... Corkran, Mary A./51/female/single/Md, Md, Md/Feb/pneumonia/51yrs in the
county
... Jewell, Anna /34/female/married/Md, Md, Del/Mar/childbrith/34 yrs in the
county/Willis
... Charles, Willis/69/male/married/Md, Md, Md/grocery merchant/Dec/enteritis/
69/Jefferson
... Bell, Joshua/68/male/Black/married/Md, Md, Md/farmer/Aug/diarrhea/68 yrs
in the county
... Nicols, Minnia/2/female/single/Md, Md, Md/Apr/Diutition(?)/2 yrs in the
county/Stafford(?)
... Fleetwood, Catharine/65/female/married/Del, Del, Del/Jul/debititz(?)/30 yrs
in the county/Jefferson
... Handy(?)/Healey(?), Thomas/70/male/married/N.Y, Ireland, Ireland/miller/
Jul/cancer of stomach/4 yrs in the county/Jefferson
... Sutherland(?), Idia/8(?)/female/single/Md, Md, Md/Dec/burns/8 yrs in the
county/Jefferson
... Shepherd, Matilda/60(?)/female/Black/widow/Md, Md, Md/housekeeper/May/ovian
tumor/60(?) yrs in the county/Jefferson
... Fleetwood, Jane/55/female/married/Del, Del, Del/house keeper/Nov/..?../35
yrs in the county/Jefferson/died in Federalsburg, Dorch Co.
... Amos, Frank/1/male/single/Md, -, -/Aug/cholera infantum

Addition to fifth district from physician register:
   Dukes, Sarah/60/female/married/Md, Md, Md/housekeeper/Jul/meningitis/
Jefferson
   Nichols, ___ /4/female/single/Md, Md, Md/Oct/diptheria/Jefferson
   Donnelly, J. O./54/male/married/Ireland, Ireland, Ireland/physician/Dec/
congestion of the brain/Thomas
   Gibson, Amanda/30/female/Black/married/Md, Md, Md/washerwoman/Jan/P.thesis
pulmonalis/Young
   Smith, Herman/0/male/single/Md, Md, Md/infant/Sep/whooping cough/Young

6th District
6   Elliott, Laura A./3/female/Black/single/Md, Md, Md/Apr/consumption/3 yrs
in the county/Williamson
18 Cephus, Lena/14 days/female/Black/Md, Md, Md/cholera infantum 14 days in
the county/Downes
50 Sweeney, Julia A./54/female/married/Ireland, Ireland, Ireland/keeping
house/May/chronic pneumonia/5 yrs in the county/died in Del/Judson
93 Cooper, Mary E./20/female/Md, Md, Md/died at home/Feb/consumption/20 yrs
in the county/P.S. Reynolds
... Price, Ida V./8/female/single/Md, Md, Md/Mar/diptheria/8 yrs in the county/
Thomas Hackett
122 Hutchins, Nicey/65(?)/female/Black/married/Md, Md, Md/servant/Jul/cancer in
right breast/65 yrs in the county/no attending physician
... Ringgold/Angie(?)/1 day/female/single/Md, Md, Md/Jul/Inauction(?)/no attending physician
... Thomas, William/88/male/Black/widower/Md, Md, Md/farmer/Mar/pneumonia/88 yrs
in the county/Hackett
... Wheeler, Mary E. 37/female/married/Md, Md, Md/keeping house/Apr/consumption/
37 yrs in the county/Hackett
... Sherwood, Emily/71/female/widow/Md, Md, Md/keeping house/Aug/brain fever/9
yrs in the county

... Smith, James C./1/male/Black/single/Md, Md, Md/Sep/cholera infantum/1 yr
in the county/Young
... ___,Mary D./17/female/single/Md, Md, Md/died at home/Jun/whooping cough/17
yrs in the county/Thomas Holt
... Smith, Charles S./24/male/single/Md, Md, Md/carpenter/Feb/consumption/24
yrs in the county/Holt
... Ringgold, Grace B./10 mos/female/single/Md, Md, Md/Jul/cerebral spinal
fever/10 mos/Holt
42 Urry, Annie A./1 mos/male/Black/single/Md, Md, Md/Feb/cerebra spinal fever/
1 mo/Downes
... Gibson, John/5 mos/male/single/Md, Md, Md/Feb/congestion of lungs/5 mos/
no attending physician
180 Fullman(?), Robert/6(?)/male Black/single/Md, Md, Md/Nov/whooping cough/6
yrs in the county/Young
... Fullman(?), Grace/1 mo/female/Black/single/Md, Md, Md/Jun/dropsy/1 mo/no
attending physician
... Rolph, Howard P./3/male/single/Md, Md, Md/Dec/cholera infantum/3 yrs in the
county/Hackett
... Young, Henrietta/10/female/Black/single/Md, Md, Md/Jun/hemmorhage/2 yrs in
the county/Holt
... B..., Samuel/1 mo/male/Black/single/Md, Md, Md/May/dysentery/1 mo in county
... Stewart, Bessie G./1/female/Black/single/Md, Md, Md/Mar/dropsy/1 yr/Young
... Johns, Matthew/58/male/Black/Md, Md, Md/laborer/Oct/brain fever/10 yrs in
the county/Downes
... Powell, Frederic(?) G./7 mos/male/single/Md, Md, Md/Jul/cholera infantum/7
months in the county/Holt
... Casson, Ellen/50(?)/female/Black/widow/Md, Md, Md/keeping house/Jun/
hemmorhage of womb/27 yrs in the county/Hackett
... Hines, William/2 mos/male/Black/single/Md, Md, Md/Jul/paralysis/2 mos in
the county/no attending physician
... Harington, Martha/1 mo/female/Black/single/Md, Md, Md/Aug/dysentery/1 month
in the county/no attending physician
... Franklin, Howard/2/male/Black/single/Md, Md, Md/Jun/measles/2 yrs in the
county/Downes
... Hammond Florence E./3 mos/female/Black/single/Md, Md, Md/Aug/erysipelas/
3 mos/no attending physician
... Ford, William A./73/male/widower/Md, Md, Md/farmer/Aug/tumor on the brain/
73 yrs in the county/Hackett
... Chase, ___/male/Black/single/Md, Md, Md/Jan/still born/no attending physician
... Downes, Edith/3/female/single/Md, Md, Md/Dec/croup/3 yrs in the county/
Hackett
... Adams, Lilly/14 days/female/single/Md, Md, Md/May/enlargement of heart/
Williamson
... Wayman, Margaret/1/female/Black/single/Md, Md, Md/May/dysentary/1 yr in
the county/G. W. Fisher

PART THREE

Records of Deaths and Births

required by the state of Maryland

1865 - 1885

Deaths
     Date of death/name/sex/color if other than white/married or single/age/
residence/occupation/place of death/place of birth/name of father/name of
mother/residence of parents/disease or cause of death/place of burial/date
of record

1867 Dec 13/Annie Ayers/female/single/4 mos/Tuckahoe Neck/Tuckahoe Neck/
Tuckahoe Neck/Francis Ayers/Sarah Ayers/Tuckahoe Neck/Tuckahoe Neck/1868
Jun 6

1868 May 6/Nancy Anderson/female/married/30/near Greensboro/farmer/near
Greensboro/Sussex Co Del/Horatio McGee/Tempest McGee/near Denton/child bed/
Greensboro/1868 May 13

1866 May 12/Benjamin Ayres/male/married/38/near Denton/farmer/Tuckahoe Neck/
Caroline Co/typhoid fever/buried at William Williams/1869 Jan 19

1866 May 6/Nancy H. Adams/female/widow/58/near Preston/died Tuckahoe Neck/
born Del/bur near Gilpins Point/1869 Jan 19

1865 Dec 8/Minnie C. Bryant/female/single/8 das/Denton/Denton/Denton/J. W.
Bryant/L. H. Bryant/Denton/convulsions/Denton/1866 Jan 3

Dec 12 1865/Rebecca A. Bowdle/female/single/19/Concord/Concord/Northwest Fork
Bridge/Henry Bowdle/Frances Ann Bowdle/Concord/consumption/Concord/1866 Jan 30

1866 Nov 13/Isaac Bailey/male/married/80(?) 6 mos 4 das/near Denton/farmer
near Denton/-/-/-/-/-/1866 Dec 1

1867 Sep 27/Joseph Baker/male/married/48/Denton/carpenter/Denton/Chester Co
Pa/-/-/-/lockjaw/Denton/1867 Dec 14

1867 Jun 17/Herbert S. Benson/male/single/4/Denton/-/Denton/Baltimore/B. F.
Benson/Maria E. Benson/Denton/congestion of the brain/At Mrs. Thomas/1868
Jan 17

1867 Nov 3/Richard Bullock/male/married/70/Smithville/farmer/Smithville/Del/
Thomas Bullock/Mary Bullock/Del/apoplexy/Bloomery Chapel/1868 Mar 24

1868 May 5/J. B. T. Benson/male/infant/2 mos/Denton/-/Denton/Denton/B. F.
Benson/M. E. Benson/Denton/-/Poplar Grove/1868 May 13

1868 Sep 4/Gertrude A. G. Baynard/female/Black/2 weeks/near Bryans Mills/-/
near Bryans Mills/near Bryans Mills/William H. Baynard/Alice Baynard/near
Bryans Mills/at John Robinson's/1868 Sep 8

1865 Aug -/Dorcas Canner/female/widow/-/Denton/weaver/Denton/-/-/-/-/
dysentery/Denton/1865 Nov 16

1866 Aug 2/Jennie Carroll/female/-/11 mos/Hubbards Crossroads/-/Hubbards
Crossroads/Hubbards Crossroads/Rossell Carroll/Lucy A. Carroll/Hubbards
Crossroads/dysentary/Concord/1866 Aug 9

1866 Oct 1/Charlie S. Corkran/male/single/6(?)/Fowling Creek/-/Fowling Creek/
Fowling Creek/Thomas F. Corkran/Mary E. Corkran/Fowling Creek/cholera
infantum/Fowling Creek/1867 Jan 8

State Records of Deaths and Births

1867 Apr 4/William Cephas/male/Black/married/38/Denton/bar keeper/near
Potters Landing /-/-/-/-/convulsions/Denton/1867 Dec 14

1867 Jan 4/___Colescott/female/married/60/near Denton/housekeeper/near Denton/
Caroline Co/-/-/-/pneumonia/Denton/1867 Dec 16

1866 Jan 27/Robert B. Comegys/male/single/60 das/near Greensborough/-/near
Greensborough/near Greensboro/William H. Comegys/Martha S. Comegys/near
Greensborough/whooping cough/Greensborough/1867 Dec 16

1867 Oct 15/Jacob Charles/male/married/87 yrs 3 mos/Federalsburg/farmer/
Federalsburg/Dorchester Co/-/-/-/old age/Federalsburg/1867 Dec 17

1868 Jan 2/Henrietta Cohee/female/married/44/near Anthony's Mills/housekeeper/
near Anthony's Mills/-/-/-/-/bronchitis/A. William Sorden's/1868 Jan 6

1867 Aug 9/Candace Carmean/female/widow/63/near Concord/housekeeper/near
Concord/Caroline Co/James J. Hubbard/Nancy Hubbard/Caroline Co/paralysis/
Concord/1868 Jan 28

1868 Jun 22/Cornelius Comegys/male/widower/70/Greensboro/merchant/Greensboro/
Caroline Co/William Comegys/Martha Comegys/Caroline Co/disease of the kidney/
Greensboro/30 Jun 1868

1869 Jan 2/Elisha Corkran/male/married/77/New Hope/shoemaker/New Hope/Caroline
Co/Henry Corkran/Lisha Corkran/Caroline Co/Eresipelar(?)/New Hope/23 Apr 1869

1869 Jul 7/Walter M. Cunningham/male/infant/7 weeks/Denton/-/Denton/Denton/
Robert Cunningham/Anna E. Cunningham/Denton/cholera infantum/Denton/1869 Nov 9

1871 Sep 9/Galena Collison/female/infant/3 mos 13 das/Tuckahoe Neck/-/Tuck
Tuckahoe Neck/Tuckahoe Neck/Robert K. Collison/Mary F. Collison/Tuckahoe Neck/
-/at home/1871 Sep 14

1866 Apr 30/Edward Hardcastle Downes/male/single/2 weeks/Denton/-/Denton/
Denton/P. W. Downes/A. H. Downes/Denton/Inanitum(?)/Denton/1867 Dec 16

1866 Apr 7/Samuel Dunning/male/married/66/near Denton/farmer/near Denton/
Caroline Co/Bachelor Chance/Taner(?) Dunning/Caroline Co/pneumonia/
Greensborough/1867 Dec 16

1866/Nov 8/Laura Draper/female/single/9/near Burrsville/-/near Burrsville/
Caroline Co/T. H. Draper/Sarah Draper/Caroline Co/typhoid fever/Greensboro/
1867 Dec 16

1867 Mar 22/John H. Dukes/male/married/47/Greensborough/farmer/Greensborough/
Caroline Co/-/-/Caroline Co/heart disease/Tuckahoe Neck/1868 Apr 20

1884 Aug 10/Louise Deakyne/female/infant/6 mos 12 das/Denton/-/Denton/Denton/
George A. Deakyne/Clara Deakyne/Denton/cholera infantum/Denton Cemetery/
1884 Aug 13

1868 Feb 22/Maria Emerson/female/married/near Denton/-/near Denton/Talbot Co/
Jonathan Evitts/-/-/-/child bed fever/Denton/1869 Mar 4

1865 Sep 4/Sarah Farfinger/female/married/50/Caroline Co/housekeeper/
Smithville/Montgomery Co Pa/George Bydman/-/Montgomery Pa/consumption/Concord/
1865 Sep 19

1865 Oct 21/Mary E. Fountain/female/widow/47/Denton/housekeeper/Denton/
Caroline Co/Abraham Jump/Lydie(?) Jump/Caroline Co/gastro enteritis/Denton/
1865 Nov 16

-80-

State Records of Deaths and Births

1868 Sep 10/Lillian Forest/female/single/age unknown/Denton/-/Denton/unknown/
unknown/unknown/unknown/consumption/near Denton/

1865 Dec -/Joseph Lincoln Griffith/male/4 yrs 10 mos/Denton/-/Denton/Denton/
Joseph Griffith/Elizabeth Griffith/Denton/croup/Denton/1866 Jul 26

1866 Jun 21/Francena Griffith/female/-/5 mos/Denton/-/Denton/Denton/Joseph
Griffith/Elizabeth Griffith/Denton/dysentary/Denton/1866 Jul 26

1867 Nov 7/Alexander Greenley/male/married/34/Hillsborough/merchant/
Hillsborough/Caroline Co/James Greenley/Mary Greenley/Caroline Co/consumption/
Hillsborough/1868 Mar 6

1868 Sep 19/Helena Green/female/-/41/near Jumptown/-/near Jumptown/Caroline
Co/John Jump of William/Mary Jump/Caroline Co/consumption/Ridgely/1864 Jan 19

1882 Aug 15/Lydia M. Gadd/female/widow/73 yrs, 6 mos, 15 das/near Jumptown/
lady/Hillsborough/Caroline Co/Abraham Jump/Sidney Carter Jump/Caroline Co/-/
Hillsboro/1883 Jan 31

1865 Sep 9/Kate Harris/female/single/24/near Denton/-/near Denton/-/John
Harris/Elizabeth Harris/near Denton/typhoid fever/near Denton/1865 Nov 16

1866 Nov 25/James H. Hubbard/male/married/29/near Harmony/farmer/near Harmony/
Caroline Co/Lemuel Hubbard/-/near Harmony/typhoid fever/near Harmony/1866
Jul 31

1867 Jun 19/Michael Hubbard/male/married/82/near Federalsburg/farmer/near
Federalsburg/Caroline Co/Thomas Hubbard/-/near Federalsburg/inflamation of
the lungs/Jesse Banning's/1867 Dec 24

1866 Aug 26/James H. Hubbard/ male/single/4 mos/Harmony/-/Harmony/Harmony/
James H. Hubbard/Catharine Hubbard/Harmony/typhoid fever/at L. Hubbard's/
1867 Dec 31

1867 Apr 30/Mary E. Humphrey/female/single/5/near Harmony/-/near Harmony/
Michigan/Daniel Humphrey/Mary Humphrey/near Harmony/bronchitis/Union Church/
1868 Jan 14

1868 Jul 2/Rebecca A. Harmon/female/widow/35 yrs, 6 mos/18 das/Caroline Co/
-/Caroline Co; Denton/Elijah Baker/Elizabeth Baker/Caroline Co/dropsy/Concord/
1868 Sep 1

1865 Sep 22/Annie Eliza Jump/female/single/1 mo, 2 das/Denton/-/Denton/Denton/
Josiah Jump/Margaret H. Jump/Denton/whooping cough/Jumptown/1866 Dec 18

1867 Apr 24/William Johnson/male/Black/single/17/near Denton/laborer/near
Denton/Greensborough/Denard Johnson/Annie Johnson/Caroline Co/plurisey/Denton/
1867 Dec 13

1866 Nov 11/Robert J. B. Joiner/male/single/24/near Denton/carpenter/near
Denton/Caroline Co/Absess liver/near Denton/1867 Dec 16

1865 Sep 20/Mary Pauline Liden/female/single/9 mos/Denton/-/Denton/Denton/
S. Fountain Liden/Annie G. Liden/Denton/cholera infantum/Denton/1865 Nov 16

1866 Oct 12/William(?) A. Liden/male/married/48/New Potters Landing/farmer/
near Potters Landing/Caroline Co/Edward Liden/-/Caroline Co/perforation of
bowels/Concord/1867 Dec 16

1868 Feb 16/__Love/male/married/-/Jumptown/farmer/Jumptown/-/......

1867/Aug 11/Laura Lehman/female/single/22 days/...Isaac Lehman/Mary A. Lehman/
Concord/1868 May 13

-81-

State Records of Deaths and Births

1868 Jan 25/Ignatius Lednum/male/married/Denton/shoemaker/Denton/-/Edward
Lednum;Lizzie Lednum/-/-/Denton/1868 Aug 25

1869 Jan 3/Roberta May Lyden/female/single/2 yrs 5 mos/Potters Landing/miller/
Denton/Potters Landing/S. Fountain Lyden/Anna G. Lyden/Potters Landing/
scarlet fever/Denton/1869 Aug 31

1866 Mar 14/Celia Maluney/female/married/47/near Denton/-/near Denton/near
Milford/-/-/Del/consumption/near Denton/1866 Apr 23

1866 Dec 23/John F. Mason/male/Black/single/36/near Denton/farmer/near Denton/
near Denton/Thomas Mason/Martha Mason/near Denton/liver disease/near Denton/
1867 Jan 7

1869 Mar 26/Ann Meloney/female/single/5(?)/near Andersontown/-/Anderstown/
near Andersontown/William Meluney/Ann Meluney/near Andersontown/measels/near
Andersontown/1869 May 4

1880 Aug 17/Marshall H. Mutchler/male/single/8 mos, 15 das/Denton/-/Denton/
Denton/Marshall S. Mutchler/Lena M. Mutchler/Denton/cholera infantum/
Greensborough/1882 Mar 15

1867 Oct 28/Horace Nicols/male/Black/single/38/Denton/laborer/Denton/Denton/
Thomas Nicols/Sarah Nicols/Denton/bilious plurisy/Denton/1867 Dec 14

1865 Sep 1/Samuel C. Ozman/male/single/2 mos/Denton/-/Denton/Denton/John H.
Ozman/Isabelle Ozman/Denton/cholera infantum/Denton 1865 Nov 16

1865 Aug 19/Henry C. Pritchett/male/single/14/Greensborough/-/Greensborough/
near Smithville/Peter B. Pritchett/Sarah Jane Pritchett/Denton/dropsy/Del/
1867 Dec 11

1867 Jun 17/Luella S. Pritchett/female/single/2/Denton/-/Denton/Denton/
Edward Pritchett/Sarah W. Pritchett/Denton/cholera infantum/Denton/1867 Dec 11

1867 Oct 10/Amelia Patton/female/married/24/near Fowling Creek/housekeeper/
Fowling Creek/Fowling Creek/Isaiah C. Blades/Milkey Blades/near Fowling Creek/
consumption/at her residence/1868 Jan 7

1867 Nov 11/Charles Peck/male/Black/married/35/near Hillsborough/farmer/near
Hillsborough/-/-/-/-/congestive fever/-/1868 Feb 1

1868 Jun 20/H. Elbert Phillip/male/Black/single/29/near Harmony/laborer/near
Harmony/near Harmony/W. Phillip/Mary Phillip/near Harmony/consumption/near
Federalsburg/1868 Aug 4

1866 Apr 13/Rolle/female/married/-/Denton/-/Denton/Germany/-/-/Germany/cancer/
.../Denton/1866 Apr 23

1873 Nov 2/James Brooks Rumbold/male/single/1 1/2/Harmony/-/Harmony/Harmony/
John Rumbold/Mary F. Rumbold/Harmony/cholera infantum/near Harmony/1873 Nov 14

1866 Jul 8/William T. Shields/male/10 mos, 12 das/Caroline Co/-/Caroline Co/
Caroline Co/Charles H. Shields/Sarah A. Shields/Caroline Co/dysentary/near
Denton/1866 Aug 9

1866 Oct 22/John Scotton/male/single/20/Caroline Co/farmer/Caroline Co/Kent
Co Del/Philemon Scotton/-/Caroline Co/typhoid fever/near..?/1867 Dec 16

1866 Aug 27/Peter Sullivan/male/married/-/near Concord/farmer/near Concord/
Concord/James Sullivan/Tamsey Sullivan/near Concord/consumption/Concord/1867
Dec 24

State Records of Deaths and Births

1867 Apr 10/Mary C. Saulsbury/female/single/6 mos/Tuckahoe Neck/farmer/
Tuckahoe Neck/Tuckahoe Neck/William E. Saulsbury/Mary J. Saulsbury/Tuckahoe
Neck/brain fever/Denton/1868 Jan 22

1866 Jul 18/William Louis Stewart/male/single/2/Hillsborough/-/Hillsborough/
Hillsborough/Joseph Stewart/Marcella Stewart/Hillsborough/dysentery/1868 Feb 1

1867 Nov 21/John Wesley Stewart/male/single/7/Hillsborough/-/Hillsborough/Wye
Landing/Joseph Stewart/Marcella Stewart/Hillsborough/rheumatism/Hillsborough/
1868 Feb 1

1867 Mar 19/Bennett Sylvester/male/widower/49/Hillsborough/shoemaker/
Hillsborough/Caroline Co/-/-/Caroline Co/pneumonia/Hillsborough/1868 Feb 1

1868 Nov 12/Thomas Ovide Smith/male/infant/1 mo, 9 days/Denton/-/Denton/
Denton/Thomas A. Smith/Sarah R. Smith/Denton/convulsions/Denton/1868 Dec 21

1866 Mar 15/Thomas Towers/male/married/41/Denton/-/shipper/Denton/Caroline Co/
-/-/Caroline Co/pneumonia/Denton/1866 Apr 23

1866 May 15 Ida Taylor/female/Black/single/6 mos/near Denton/-/near Denton/
Caroline Co/T. N. Taylor/Elizabeth Taylor/Caroline Co/headfall/Denton/1867
Dec 19

1866 Jun 19/Zebdial Taylor/male Black/single/2 yrs, 6 mos/near Denton/near
Denton/Caroline Co/T. N. Taylor/Elizabeth Taylor/Caroline Co/billious
dysentery/Denton/1867 Dec 19

1868 Sep 3/Jonathan Tylor/male/married/61 yrs, 8 mos/Denton/trader/Denton/
Caroline Co/Thomas Tylor/-/Caroline Co/congestive chill/near Denton/1869
Mar 29

1868 Jan 20/Sarah Turner/female/widow/62/Fowling Creek/housekeeper/Fowling
Creek/near Federalsburg/-/-/-/general debility/Preston/1869 Dec 14

1866 Apr 2/William Urry/male/widower/79/Caroline Co/farmer/Tuckahoe Neck/
Caroline Co/Thomas Urry/Mary Urry/Caroline Co/consumption/Concord/1866 Apr 10

1866 Aug 24/Laura Virginia Urry/female/-/7 mos, 7 das/Caroline Co/near Denton/
Caroline Co/Thomas L. Urry/Adah M. Urry/Caroline Co/-/Concord/1866 Aug 28

1865 Jul 14/Robert Henry Voss/male/single/8/Denton/-/Denton/Denton/Holliday
Voss/Nancy E. Voss/Denton/dysentery/near Union Corner/1865 Jul 20

1865 Aug 26/James Willard Willson/male/single/16 das/near Denton/-/near
Denton/near Denton/James H.(?) Wilson/Susan Wilson/Caroline Co/cholera
infantum/near Denton/1866 Jan 30

1867 Mar 5/Elizabeth E. Waddell/female/married/18 yrs, 3 mos/near Preston/-/
near Preston/near Denton/Robert K. Collison/Catharine Collison/Caroline Co/
convulsions/Preston/1867 Apr 6

1867 Aug 28/William Ellwood Waddle/male/single/5 mos, 25 das/near Preston/-/
near Preston/near Preston/William B. Waddle/Elizabeth E. Waddle/Caroline Co/
cholera infantum/Preston/1867 Sep 7

1867 Jul 27/George M. Whitby/male/married/27/Bridgetown/farmer/near
Bridgetown/near Denton/James M. Whitby/ Catharine Whitby/Caroline Co/soften-
ing of the brain/near Greensboro/1869 Dec 17

1867 Nov 30/William E. Whitby/male/single/4 yrs, 9 mos/near Bridgetown/-/near
Bridgetown/near Greensboro/George M. Whitby/Sarah M. Whitby/Caroline Co/
diptherea/near Greensboro/1867 Dec 17

State Records of Deaths and Births

1867 Dec 12/Frederick L. Whitby/male/single/3 yrs, 2 1/2 mos/Bridgetown/-/
near Bridgetown/near Greensboro/George M. Whitby/Sarah M. Whitby/Caroline
Co/dipthera/near Greensboro/1867 Dec 17

1867 Sep 14/James H. Willoughby/male/single/22/near Harmony/farmer/near
Harmony/Hunting Creek/William Willoughby/Elizabeth C. Willoughby/Caroline
Co/typhoid fever/Union Grove/1867 Dec 17

1867 Jul 18/Rebecca E. Wright/female/single/21/near Smithville/housekeeper/
near Smithville/near Smithville/Peter Wright/Priscilla Wright/near Smithville/
consumption/Bloomery/1867 Dec 24

1868 Jan 19/Robert Emmet Whitby/male/single/6 yrs, 10 mos/near Greensboro/
-/near Greensboro/near Greensboro/James M. Whitby/Catharine Whitby/near
Greensboro/diptherea/Greensboro/1868 Feb 3

1867 Sep 10/John W. Williams/male/single/18/Friendship/farmer/Hunting Creek/
Baynard Williams/Sarah Williams/near Friendship/drowned at M. Williams/1868
Feb 3

1868 Nov 29/William Williams/male/widower/61/Tuckahoe Neck/farmer/Tuckahoe
Neck/Del/Henry Williams/Lydia Williams/Tuckahoe Neck/-/his residence/1869
Jan 19

1869 Jan 1/Henry Williams/male/-/4/Tuckahoe Neck/Tuckahoe Neck/William A.
Williams/Caroline Williams/Tuckahoe Neck/mumps/William Williams/1869 May 11

1868 Jan 31/__Wright/male/-/12 das/near Smithville/-/near Smithville/near
Smithville/Lewis B. Wright/Sarah Wright/near Smithville/-/near Smithville
1869 Sep 21

1869 Nov (?)/Henry Willis/male/single/48/Fowling Creek/farmer/near Fowling
Creek/near Preston/Peter Willis/Mary Ann Willis/near Fowling Creek/
consumption/Fowling Creek/1871 Apr 8

1868 Jul 18/Mary E. Wright/female/married/44/near Preston/farmer/near
Preston, Dorch Co/Garretson McBride/Susan McBride/Dorch Co/typhoid fever/
Salem, Dorch Co/1870 Sep 23

1868 Aug 4/Daniel E. Wright/male/single/10 mos/near Preston/farmer(sic)/near
Vienna, Dorch Co/near Preston/Daniel R. Wright/Mary E. Wright/near Preston/
diarrhea/Salem, Dorch Co/1870 Sep 23

1882 Apr 15/Alfred L. Warren/male/married/46/Linchester/-/Linchester/Prince
Edwards Island/William Warren/Mary Warren/England/bronchitis/cemetery of
Jesse Hubbard/1882 Apr 13

1867 Jul 2/Maggie Benson/female/single/9 mos/Denton/Denton/-/B.F. Benson/
Maria E. Benson/Denton/Congestion of the brain/at Mrs. Thomas 1868 Jan 77

State Records of Deaths and Births

<u>Births</u>
    Date of birth/place of birth/name/sex/color if other than white/father/
mother/occupation of parent/date of record

1867 Jan 2/near Denton/Elissa Emily Andrew/female/Peter Andrew/Mary Ellen
Andrew/farmer/1868 Jan 7

1866 Jul 7/near Ridgely Station/Charles Ridgley Allison/male/Robert C.
Allison/Ellen Eliza Allison/teacher/1868 Jun 9

1868 May 8/near Ridgely Station/Effie Leora Allison/female/Robert C. Allison/
Ellen Eliza Allison/teacher/1868 Jun 9

1868 Jul 14/near Denton/Peter Andrew/male/Peter Andrew/Mary Ellen Andrew/
laborer/1868 Sep 29

1869 Feb 5/near Denton/·__/male/William Argo/Mary Argo/farmer/1869 Mar 4

1865 Jul 17/Smithville/William Edward Bullock/male/William H. Bullock/Rebecca
C. Bullock/farmer/1865 Oct 16

1865 Sep 1/near Denton/Mary C. Butler/female/James H. Butler/Mary C. Butler/
laborer/1865 Nov 16

1865 Dec 1/Denton/Minnie C. Bryant/female/J. W. Bryant/L. H. Bryant/lawyer/
1866 Jan 3

1865 Sep 16/Concord/Robert A. Bowdle/male/Henry Bowdle/Frances Ann Bowdle/
farmer/1866 Jan 30

1866 Apr 8/near Denton/·__/female/Josiah A. Beck/Martha E. Beck/laborer/1866
Apr 23

1865 Dec 25/near Hillsborough/Robert E. Bell/Isaac J. Bell/Wilhemina Bell/
farmer/1866 Jun 19

1867 Jul 7/near Denton/Linna T. Bryant/female/Joshua W. Bryant/Sallie H.
Bryant/lawyer/1867 Jul 15

1861 Jul 21/Centreville/Howard Bryant/male/Joshua W. Bryant/Sallie H. Bryant/
lawyer/1867/Jul 15

1867 Nov 8/near Harmony/Irva Butler/male/Peter W. Butler/Martha E. Butler/
farmer/1867 Dec 10

1866 Apr 8/near Denton/Ida Cornelia Barber/female/Black/William Barber/Cusby
Barber/laborer/1867 Dec 14

1866 Aug 24/near Concord/Anne E. Beachamp/female/James Beachamp/Rebecca
Beachamp/farmer/1867 Dec 21

1866 Sep 10/near Greensborough/Frances Ann Butler/female/James H. Butler/
Maria Catharine Butler/farmer/1868 Jan 7

1867 Aug 21/near Greensborough/Charles Henry Bell/Andrew F. Bell/Fannie Bell/
farmer/1868 Feb 4

1867 Feb 8/___/George H. Booker/male/William W. Booker/Martha T. Booker/-/
1868 Feb 6

1867 Nov 11/near Preston/Martin L. Wright/male/Levein Wright/Sarah Wright/
farmer/1868 Mar 12 (Note that this entry is out of alphabetical sequence.)

1868 Feb 17/Denton/John Baynard Thomas Benson/B. F. Benson/M. E. Benson/
preacher/1868 May 14

Births

1866 Sep 4/Greensborugh/Samuel Boothe/male/James A. Boothe/Elizabeth E. Boothe/carpenter/1868 Jun 23

1868 Aug 31/near Bryans Mill/Gertrude Atsadore Guionis Baynard/female/Black/ William Baynard/Alice Baynard/sailor/1868 Sep 8

1868 May 12/Concord Church/Anna V. Bowdel/female/Henry Bowdel/Francis A. Bowdel/-/1868 Oct 6

1868 Oct 7/near Denton/-/male/William R. Butler/farmer/1869 Mar 4

1869 Sep 13/near Greensboro/Charles H. Brown/John C. Brown/Rachel E. Brown/ farmer/1869 Sep 15

1869 Oct 4/Denton/Joseph Kent Cook Bryant/J. W. Bryant/Sallie H. Bryant/ lawyer/1870 Mar 14

1870 Jun 3/near Smithville/Richard James Shadrick Bullock/male/William H. Bullock/Rebecca C. Bullock/farmer/1870 Dec 20

1878 Apr 7/Hillsborough/Claude Jump Brown/male/J. Thomas Brown/Nora Brown/ mechanic/1880 Dec 7

1870 Nov 8/near Andersontown/Richard John Butler/male/James A. Butler/ Elizabeth K. Butler/farmer/1880 Dec 7

1872 Nov 18/near Andersontown/Eliza Ann Butler/female/James A. Butler/ Elizabeth K. Butler/farmer/1880 Dec 7

1875 Mar 22/near Andersontown/Mary Catharine Butler/female/James A. Butler/ Elizabeth K. Butler/farmer/1880 Dec 7

1865 Nov 21/Federalsburg/George Walter Connelly/male/Zacharias Connelly/Mary E. Connelly/farmer/1866 Apr 17

1866 Apr 16/near Denton/___/female/Peter Coble/Annie E. Coble/farmer/1866 Apr 23

1865 Sep 8/Hubbards Crossroads/Jennie Caroll/female/Russel W. Caroll/Lucy A. Caroll/farmer/1866 Apr 24

1866 Apr 28/near Denton/Charles Collison/male/Robert K. Collison/Mary F. Collison/farmer/1866 Aug 4

1866 Apr 14/near Harmony/Charles Summerfield Corkran/male/Thomas F. Corkran/ Mary E. Corkran/1866 Aug 30

1866 Oct 7/Hubbards Crossroads/James Martin Caroll/male/Russell W. Caroll/ Lucy A. Caroll/farmer/1867 Feb 19

1866 Oct 8/Glenwood/Samuel J. Carroll/male/George W. Carroll/Margaret E. Carroll/farmer/1867 Mar 19

1866 Apr 16/near Denton/Ida May Coble/female/Peter Coble/Annie E. Coble/ farmer/1867 Dec 16

1865 Oct 19/near Greensborough/Norman Flemming Comegys/male/William W. Comegys/Martha S. Comegys/farmer/1867 Dec 16

1866 Nov 29/near Greensborough/Robert Beatly Comegys/male/William W. Comegys/ Martha S. Comegys/farmer/1867 Dec 16

State Records of Deaths and Births

Births

1866 Sep 15/near Bethlehem/Walter Thomas Chase/male/Black/Hezekiah Chase/
Julia Ann Chase/laborer/1868 Feb 15

1867 Apr 20/Union Corner/William Tilghman Harvey Collison/male/William Edward
Collison/Sarah Elizabeth Collison/mechanic/1868 Feb 15

1867 Apr 30/Greensborough/Robert Bently Comegys/male/Col William H. Comegys/
Martha S. Comegys/farmer/1868 Jun 20.

1869 Feb 7/Greensborough/Henry Carter/male/Peter Coble/Anna E. Coble/farmer/
1869 Mar 4.

1869 Jan 1/Fowling Creek/Emma Frances Corkran/female/Solomon B. Corkran/
Mary E. Corkran/farmer/1869/May 25

1869 May 19/Denton/Walter Morris Cunningham/male/Robert W. Cunningham/ Anna
E. Cunningham/mechanic/1869 Nov 9

1869 Aug 24/ Tuckahoe Neck/Benjamin Franklin Collison/male/Robert K. Collison/
Mary F. Collison/farmer/1870 Feb 17

1870 Oct 28/Wilmington Del/Sallie E. Conrad/female/Aaron Conrad/Ary Ann
Conrad/farmer/1859 Oct 30

1871 May 27/Tuckahoe Neck/Gallena Collison/female/Robert K. Collison/Mary F.
Collison/farmer/1871 Sep 14

1853 Apr 19/Centreville/Clinton Cook/male/Clinton Cook/Maretta Cook/lawyer/
1874 Mar 25

1877 Jul 12/Denton/Bessie Russell Cook/female/Clinton Cook/Sadie L. Cook/
clerk/1879 Jun 21

1866 Apr 9/near Denton/___/male/John R. Dick/Mary Dick/farmer/1866 Apr 23

1866 Apr 15/Denton/Edward Hardcastle Downes/male/Philip W. Downes/Annie H.
Downes/lawyer/1866 Apr 23

1867 May 1/Fowling Creek/Clara Bell Dukes/female/Charles G. Dukes/Sarah E.
Dukes/1867 Oct 28

1867 Feb 4/near Denton/Charles Griffith Dukes/male/J. Boon Dukes/Melissa
Dukes/farmer/1867 Dec 16

1867 Apr 28/Denton/Raymond Worthington Downes/male/J.W. Downes/Annie H.
Downes/lawyer/1867 Dec 16

1868 Jul 12/near Denton/Charles Percival Dunning/male/Charles A. Dunning/
Ella M. Dunning/farmer/1869 Jan 14

1868 May 10/near Denton/____/female/John B. Dukes/Maria L. Dukes/farmer/1869
Mar 4

1868 Dec 18/Denton/___/male/Philip W. Downes/Anna H. Downes/lawyer/1869 Mar 4

1869 Nov 20/Hillsborough/Anna E. Duffey/female/Hugh Duffey/Catharine Duffey/
druggist/1874 Jan 13

1869 Jan 4/Hillsborough/Hugh Clarence Duffey/male/Hugh Duffey/Catharine
Duffey/druggist/1874 Jan 13

1872 Apr/Hillsborough/Catharine Lee Duffey/female/Hugh Duffey/Catharine
Duffey/druggist/1874 Jan 13

1876 Dec 1/Greensborough/Lola W. Downes/female/William T. Downes/Louisianna
Downes/mechanic/1880 Dec 7

State Records of Deaths and Births

Births

1857 Sep 11/Smyrna Del/George A. Deakyne/male/George A. Deakyne/Elmira
Deakyne/farmer/1884 Aug 13

1884 Jan 29/Denton/Louise Deakyne/female/George A. Deakyne/Clara Deakyne/
deputy clerk/1884 Aug 13

1863 Nov 4/near Smithville/Litha Jane Eaton/female/Ezekiel Eaton/Levice Ann
Eaton/farmer/1866 Feb 6

1866 Jan 20/Potters Landing/Nancy Bell Eaton/female/William Eaton/Marietta
Eaton/laborer/1866 Sep 4

1866 Jul 30/near Brick Mill/Jacob Spencer Eaton/male/Black/George Eaton/
Wilmina Eaton/laborer/1867 Dec 30

1866 Sep 22/Hubbards Crossroads/John Lee Everngam/male/Joseph H. Everngam/
Martha Everngam/farmer/1868 Jan 28

1868 Jul 13/Mullica Hill N.J./Lizzie Roberta Emerson/female/J. Marion Emerson/
Lizzie S. Emerson/printer/1869 Jan 12

1868 Feb 10/near Denton___/male/Robert R. Emerson/Maria Emerson/farmer/1869
Mar 4

1870 Dec 13/Denton/John Clarence Emerson/male/John H. Emerson/Rebecca A.
Emerson/editor/1872 Jan 9

1871 Sep 28/Tuckahoe Neck/Mary W. Evitts/female/Jonathan Evitts/Williamina
Evitts/sheriff/1872 Jul 20

1873 Nov 13/Denton/Mary Luretta Emerson/female/John H. Emerson/Rebecca A.
Emerson/1874 Jan 13

1865 Oct 7/near Denton/Thomas Francis Flowers/male/James H. Flowers/Lucinda
Flowers/farmer/1866 Jan 30

1866 Feb 9/3rd election district/William J. Fell/male/William Fell/Henrietta
Fell/farmer/1867 Dec 16

1866 Jul 16/Denton/Bradley J. Fisher/male/T. W. Fisher/Annie W. Fisher/
merchant/1867 Dec 16

1866/near Denton/Mary C. Cline/female/David L. Cline/Sidney A. Cline/salesman/
1867 Dec 16

1867 Dec 23/near Smithville/Ellen H. Favinger/female/David Favinger/Mary W.
Favinger/farmer/1868 Feb 3

1867 Oct 16/near Harmony/Mary Ida Friend/female/Black/Francis Friend/Ruth
Friend/farmer/1868 Dec 15

1868 Feb 11/near Keens Landing/Charles Fell/male/William Fell/Henrietta Fell/
farmer/1868 Dec 18

1866 Mar 23/near Denton/___/male/Matthew Garey/Sarah J. Garey/farmer/1866
Apr 23

1866 Feb 15/Denton/Franena Griffith/female/Joseph Griffith/Elizabeth Griffith/
carpenter/1866 Jul 26

1866 Mar 23/near Denton/Matthew Garey/male/Matthew Garey/Sarah Jane Garey/
farmer/1866 Aug 11

State Records of Death and Birth

<u>Birth</u>

1866 Aug 13/near Potters Landing/James W. Griffith/male/Aaron A. Griffith/ Candas R. Griffith/farmer/1867 Jan 28

1866 Nov 26/near Hillsborough/Lydia Augusta Green/female/Foster Green/Jane E. Green/farmer/1867 Apr 1

1867 Oct 16/near Burrsville/___/female Black/William Grinage/farmer/1867 Dec 16

1867 Nov 18/Hillsborough/Alexander Horsey Greenley/female?/Alexander Greenley/ Anna D. Greenley/merchant/1868 Mar 6

1869 Mar 6/near Concord/Carie J. Griffith/female/Aaron A. Griffith/Candice R. Griffith/farmer/1869 Aug 3

1867 Jun 11/Denton/Charles Desley Griffith/male/Joseph Griffith/Elizabeth Griffith/carpenter/1870 Feb 4

1869 Dec 28/Denton/John Franklin Griffith/male/Joseph Griffith/Elizabeth Griffith/carpenter/1870 Feb 4

1873 Dec 13/Denton/Elijah Griffith/male/Joseph Griffith/Elizabeth Griffith/ carpenter/1874 Aug 15

1873 Dec 7/Denton/Lafenia Griffith/female/Alexander Griffith/Rebecca Griffith/ laborer/1874 Aug 15

1865 Oct 17/near Denton/Charles Lake Harmon/male/John Wesley Harmon/Rebecca A. Harmon/farmer/1866 Apr 13

1866 Apr 23/near Denton/___/male/John Horsey/Ruth Horsey/farmer/1866 Apr 23

1866 Apr 17/near Harmony/James Henry Hubbard/male/James H. Hubbard/Nancy C. Hubbard/farmer/1866 Jul 31

1867 Jun 12/near Harmony/Mary Virginia Hutchinson/female/A. L. Hutchinson/ Wilmina Hutchinson/laborer/1867 Dec 10

1866 Dec 4/near Concord/Wenna Blades Hubbard/female/James P. T. Hubbard/ Martha Hubbard/farmer/1868 Jan 28

1865 Mar 9/Hillsborough/Margaret N. Hackett/female/Dr. Thomas Hackett/ Margaret B. Hackett/physician/1868 Feb 1

1868 Apr 16/Caroline Co/John Wesley Harmon/male/John W. Harmon/Rebecca A. Harmon/farmer/1868 Sep 7

1868 Mar 15/Hillsborough/Charles Hill Hammersley/male/James W. Hammersley/ Anna W. Hammersley/minister/1868 Sep 7

1860 Jun 16/Denton/Clara Horsey/female/William G. Horsey/Maria Louise Horsey/ farmer/1884 Aug 13

1865 Nov 14/Tuckahoe Neck/Luther Marion Jewell/male/Luther M. Jewell/Julia A. Jewell/farmer/Jan 27 1866

1865 Sep 6/Smithville/Williard Edward Johnson/male/William T. Johnson/ Elizabeth Johnson/farmer/1866 May 23

1866 Aug 29 near Denton/Sarah Jane Garey Joiner/female/William Joiner/Mary Jane Joiner/farmer/1866 Dec 4

1865 Aug 20/Denton/Annie Eliza Jump/female/Josiah Jump/Margaret H. Jump/clerk of Circuit Court/1866 Dec 18

State Records of Death and Birth

Birth

1868 Sep 5/Piney Grove/Frances Elizabeth Joiner/female/William Joiner/Mary J. Joiner/farmer/1869 Mar 4

1868 May 19/near Denton/___/female(?)/Henry Irvin/_/farmer/1869 Mar 4

1867 Nov 5/near Concord/George Bascom Jenkins/male/__/Rebecca Jenkins/house servant/1869 May 11

1865 Oct 19/Denton/Grace R. Kemp/female/Iben(?) D. Kemp/M. Virginia Kemp/ lawyer/1865 Nov 16

1865 Oct 26/Denton/Margaret Petersen Kemp/female/Thomas H. Kemp/Sallie E. Kemp/lawyer/1865 Nov 16

1866 Oct 23/Hillsborough/Mary Kemp/female/Charles B. Kemp/Elizabeth J. Kemp/ sailor/1868 Feb 1

1865 Apr 1/Hillsborough/Laura Elma Kemp/female/Charles B. Kemp/Elizabeth J. Kemp/sailor/1868 Feb 1

1868 Feb 29/Denton/Thomas H. Kemp the 3rd/male/Thomas Kemp Jr/Sarah E. Kemp/ clerk of the Circuit Court/1868 Jun 30

1868 Dec 25/near Denton/___/female/A. Y. Knisely/Anna Knisely/farmer/1869 Mar 4

1865 Nov 2/near Smithville/William F. Liden/male/William E. Liden/Vivletta Liden/farmer/1866 Jan 23

1866 Mar 1/near Denton/___/female/Luff Lewis/Rebecca Lewis/farmer/1866 Apr 23

1865 Oct 21/Greensborough/Howard M. Lank/male/Robert J. Lank/Sarah J. Lank/ merchant/1866 Jun 19

1866 Aug 4/Potters Landing/Roberta May Lyden/female/S.F. Lyden/A. G. Lyden/ miller/1867 Dec 16

1866 Dec 20/near Hunting Creek/Atley Eldredge Lord/male/Robert Lord/Mary E. Lord/farmer/1868 Mar 10

1867 Jul 20/Pennsylvania/Laura Lehman/Isaac Lehman/Mary Ann Lehman/-/1868 May 13

1867 Jul 5/Denton/Robert Ignatius Lednum/male/James I. Lednum/Alexine Lednum/ post master/1868 Aug 25

1868 Apr 3/near Smithville/Sarah R. Liden/female/William E. Liden/Violetta Liden/farmer/1868 Nov 5

1869 Jun 19/Potters Landing/Frederick Fountain Liden/male/S. Fountain Liden/ Anna G. Liden/miller/1869 Aug 31

1865 Nov 22/Smithville/Samuel Townsend Meredith/male/Dr. William H. Meredith/ Sarah S. Meredith/physician/1865 Dec 12

1867 Feb 24/Potters Landing/Oscar Willis Messick/male/Robert M. Messick/ Caroline S. Messick/merchant/1867 Apr 30

1858 Dec 27/near Andersontown/Charles K. Messick/male/Lewis Messick/Elizabeth Messick/farmer/1867 Jul 5

1862 Mar 21/near Andersontown/Lear Elizabeth Messick/female/Lewis Messick/ Elizabeth Messick/farmer/1867 Jul 5

State Records of Death and Birth

Birth

1864 Jun 10/near Andersontown/Mary Alice Messick/female/Lewis Messick/ Elizabeth Messick

1867 Jul 14/Smithville/John Meredith/male/Dr. William H. Meredith/Sarah S. Meredith/physician/1867 Dec 10

1867 Feb 4/near Andersontown/William Andrew Meluney/male/William Meluney/Ann Meluney/farmer/1867 Dec 14

1867 Feb 18/Denton/William George Miller/male/Black/Ezekiel Miller/Mary Miller/laborer/1868 Jan 2

1866 Dec 13/Hillsborough/William Wallace Mansfield/male/S. H. W. Mansfield/ Anna E. Mansfield/carpenter/1868 Feb 17

1867 Dec 4/near Denton/Otts Emanuel Miller/male/Benjamin Miller/Margaret Miller/millwright/1868 Jun 22

1867 Dec 4/near Denton/Ida Florence Miller/female/Benjamin Miller/Margaret Miller/millwright/1868 Jun 22

1868 May 23/Andersontown/Nimrod Meluney/male/William Meluney/Ann Meluney/ farmer/1868 Jul 10

1868 Feb 21/Tuckahoe Neck/___/female/Bayard Meluney/Ann Meluney/farmer/1869 Mar 4

1869 Jul 30/Smithville/Charles S. Meredith/male/W. H. Meredith/Sarah S. Meredith/physician/1869 Sep 21

1867 Jan 22/Cherry Hill, near Greensborough/William Boon Massey/male/James Massey/Sarah Rebecca Massey/merchant/1870 Oct 24

1878 Aug 25 Denton/Elsie Chattle Melvin/female/George Thomas Melvin/M. Lula Melvin/lawyer and editor/1880 Dec 7

1879 Dec 3/Denton/Marshall Hardcastle Mutchler/male/Marshall S. Mutchler/Lena M. Mutchler/lawyer and editor/1882 Mar 15

1865 Jun 13/Andersontown/Emma Nuttle/female/Tilghman Nuttle/Elizabeth Nuttle/ farmer/1864 Feb 6

1865 Oct 1/Federalsburg/Jesse Francis Neal/male/William Neal/Elizabeth A. Neal/school teacher/1866 Apr 3

1865 Oct 25/Bloomery/William T. Nicolls/male/Washington A. Nicolls/Martha Nicolls/farmer/1866 Apr 10

1868 Jan 2/Wrights Grove/William W. Noble/male/Clement Noble/Hester A. Noble/ farmer/1868 Mar 24

1868 Dec 12/Denton/___/female/Robert A. Nicolls/Mary Nicolls/mail contractor/ 1869 Mar 4

1849 Feb 25/Adams Landing/Frank E. Nichols/male/John Nichols/Elizabeth Nichols/merchant/1876 Oct 18

1865 Jul 3/Denton/Samuel Ozmon/male/John H. Ozmon/Isabelle Ozmon/sailor/1865 Jul 20

1870 Sep 28/Greensborough/Elma J. Orrell/female/Robert J. Orrell/Anna E. Orrell/farmer/1874 Jan 13

91

State Records of Death and Birth

Birth

1866 Feb 25/near Denton/John Purt/male/J. M. Purt/Emma Purt/farmer/1866 Apr 23

1866 Mar 11/near Preston/Elizabeth Emily Patton/female/Matthew L. Patton/
Gerlia E. Patton/farmer/1866 Jun 18

1866 May 29/near Harmony/Daniel Irving Patchett/male/Peter J. Patchett/Celia
Ann Patchett/farmer/1866 Oct 23

1867 Nov 6/Denton/___Pritchett/male/Edward Pritchett/Millie Pritchett/under-
taker/1867 Dec 16

1867 Jun 7/near Denton/Mary Frances Price/female/William M. Price/Eliza Jane
Price/farmer/1868Apr 21

1867 Jul 17/Greensborough/John Dukes Plummer/male/Risdon Plummer/Mary E.
Plummer/teacher/1868 Apr 21

1870 Apr 11/near Preston/Leona Patchett/female/Peter J. Patchett/Celia A.
Patchett/farmer/1870 Sep 23

1870 Oct 28/Denton/Dillie Pritchett/female/Edward Pritchett/Dillie Pritchett/
farmer/

1865 Jul 25/Burrsville/Rebecca A. Richardson/female/James T. Richardson/
Rebecca A. Richardson/laborer/1865 Nov 16

1866 Feb 18/Smithville/Annie L. Roe/female/Thomas Roe/Laura B. Roe/miller/
1866 Oct 2

1867 Aug 20/Harmony/John Rumbold/male/John Rumbold/Frances Rumbold/merchant/
1867 Dec 10

1866 Dec 3/near Denton/Charles Grant Ross/male/Black/Enoch Ross/Rachael Ross/
farmer/1867 Dec

1866 Dec 3/near Denton/Elizabeth Douglass Ross/female/Black/Enoch Ross/Rachael
Ross/farmer/1867 Dec

1867 Feb 1/Denton/___/male/F. Roshy/Sallie Roshy/shoemaker/1867 Dec 16

1866 Dec 27/Philadelphia/William Worth Ridgely/male/William S. Ridgely/Ann
Wright Ridgely/atty at law/1868 Jan 18

1868 Jan 16/near Smithville/Edward Clayton Roe/male/Thomas Roe/Laura B. Roe/
miller/1868 May 6

1868 Dec 17/Denton/___/male/Frederick Roshy/Sallie Roshy/shoemaker/1869 Mar 4

1869 Oct 17/near Fowling Creek/female/Mary Frances Rumbold/John Rumbold/Mary
F. Rumbold/farmer/1869 Nov 9

1869 Dec 18 near Denton Bridge/Francis Peercy Ridgely/male/William S. Ridgely/
Ann Acorta Ridgely/lawyer/1870 Jan 25

1872 Mar 27/Harmony/James Brook Rumbold/male/John Rumbold/Mary F. Rumbold/
farmer Oct 28___

1874 Jul 24/Harmony/Isaiah Willis Rumbold/male/John Rumbold/Mary F. Rumbold/
farmer/Aug 29 ___

1841 Apr 4/Marblehead/John Boon Ryner/male/James C. Ryner/Louise Ryner/farmer/
1875 Mar 25

1877 Feb 11/Harmony/Elizabeth Margaret Rumbold/female/John Rumbold/Mary F.
Rumbold/farmer/1877 Aug 28

State Records of Deaths and Births

Births

1879 Dec 8/Harmony/Ruth Rumbold/female/John Rumbold/Mary F. Rumbold/farmer/
1881 Feb 14

1882 Oct 2/Preston/Wade Rumbold/male/John Rumbold/Mary F. Rumbold/carpenter/
1882 Dec 2

1865 Oct 1/near Potters Landing/Benjamin Lincoln Stevens/male/William Stevens/
Unity E. Stevens/farmer/1865 Dec 19

1865 Nov 25/near Denton/ Emma Grant Saulsbury/female/James K. Saulsbury/Mary
E. Saulsbury/merchant/1865 Dec 22

1865 Nov 25/near Denton/Amanda Douglas/female/James K. Douglas/Mary E.
Douglas/merchant/1865 Dec 22

1865 Aug 26/Tuckahoe Neck/William Thomas Shields/male/Charles H. Shields/Sarah
Ann Shields/farmer/1866 Jan 30

1865 Sep 24/Tuckahoe Neck/Mary Clara Saulsbury/female/William Edward
Saulsbury/Mary Jane Saulsbury/farmer/1866 Jan 30

1865 Aug 8/near Denton/Estella Martin Stafford/female/John M. Stafford/Anna
Maria Stafford/farmer/1866 Jun 30

1866 Apr 9/near Denton/Addison Russell Smith/male/Hillman Smith/Sarah J.
Smith/farmer/1866 Apr 23

1866 Feb 6/near Denton/Robert Ernest Smith/male/Sylvester Smith/Mary Smith/
farmer/1866 May 22

1866 Mar 1/near Preston/Ida M. Satterfield/female/Elijah Satterfield/Rachael
Satterfield/farmer/1866 Aug 14

1866 Dec 31/Potters Landing/Minetta Virginia Stevens/female/Benjamin G.
Stevens/Mary V. Stevens/merchant/1867 Jun 27

1866 May 16/Denton/___/male/Alex Stewart/Elizabeth Stewart/merchant/1867 Dec 16

1867 Dec 10/Bloomery/Lemmon Catrup Slaughter/male/William S. Slaughter/Phebe
Ann Slaughter/vetinary surgeon/1868 Jan 14

1867 Jun 9/Tuckahoe Neck/Ellie Saulsbury/female/William E. Saulsbury/Mary J.
Saulsbury/farmer/1868 Jan 22

1868 Jan 23/Hillsborough/Ida Elizabeth Stewart/Joseph Stewart/Marcella
Stewart/carpenter/1868 Feb 1

1767(sic)/Union Corner/Anna Venora Stevens/female/William B. Stevens/Sarah A.
Stevens/farmer/1868 Mar 6

1867 Oct 3/Fowling Creek/James Wesley Stack/male/Frederick Stack/Mary A.
Stack/mechanic/1868 Mar 13

1868 Apr 7/Greensborough/William Henry Sipple/male/William H. Sipple/Nicey H.
Sipple/-/1868 Nov 24

1868 Oct 3/Denton/Thomas Ovide Smith/male/Thomas A. Smith/Sarah R. Smith/
carriage maker/1868 Dec 21

1868 Oct 31/Tuckahoe Neck/Anna Olevia Shields/female/Charles H. Shields/
Sally Ann Shields/farmer/1869 Mar 2

1868 Feb 23/near Denton/___/female/John Stevens/___/farmer/1869 Mar 4

Births

1868 May 13/near Andersontown/___/female/Hellman Smith/Sarah J. Smith/farmer/
1869 Mar 4

1865 May 28/near Smithville/Francis Stevens/male/John Stevens/Mary C. Stevens/
farmer/1869 Apr 1

1866 Sep 5/near Andersontown/James R. Stevens/male/John Stevens/Mary C.
Stevens/farmer/1869 Apr 1

1868 Feb 23/near Andersontown/Elizabeth Stevens/female/John Stevens/Mary C.
Stevens/farmer/1869 Apr 1

1868 Feb 2/at William A. Williams/Linda Smith/female/Black/-/Hester A. Smith/
house servant/1869 May 11

1869 Aug 25/Fowling Creek/Frederick Stack/male/Frederick Stack/Mary A. Stack/
mechanic/1869 Nov 9

1871 Mar 10/Tuckahoe Neck/James Henry Shields/male/Charles H. Shields/Sarah
A. Shields/farmer/1871 Nov 21

1865 Oct 4/near Denton/Charles Tubbs/male/David H. Tubbs/Lavernia J. Tubbs/
farmer/1865 Nov 16

1865 Nov 5/near Preston/Mary H. Towers/female/Andrew Towers/Nancy Towers/
farmer/1866 Apr 19

1867 Jan 1/Harmony/Alvey B. Todd/male/Francis S. Todd/Elizabeth Todd/farmer/
1867 Jun 15

1863 Dec 7/Harmony/Gootee S. Todd/male/Francis S. Todd/Elizabeth Todd/farmer/
1867 Jun 15

1866 May 15/near Denton/Ida Taylor/female/Black/Thomas H. Taylor/Elizabeth
Taylor/farmer/1867 Dec 19

1867 Jun 30/near Denton/Elizabeth E. Taylor/female/Thomas H. Taylor/Elizabeth
Taylor/farmer/1867 Dec 19

1866 Feb 22/near Denton/George Willson Todd/male/Robert W. Todd/Margaretta C.
Todd/farmer/1867 Dec 21

1868 Jan 27/near Union Corner/Richard Jonathan Tucker/male/John W. Tucker/
Sarah M. Tucker/farmer/1868 Feb 14

1866 Jan 17/Tuckahoe Neck/Laura Virginia Urry/female/Thomas L. Urry/Ader M.
Urry/farmer/1866 Mar 6

1865 Sep 3/near Hillsborough/Maggie Saulsbury Willson/female/Robert W. Wilson/
Carrie K. Wilson/farmer/1865 Nov 16

1865 Oct 28/Potters Landing/Sarah A. Whitaker/female/Jacob Whitaker/Sarah A.
Whitaker/farmer/1865 Nov 16

1865 Aug 10/near Denton/James Willard Willson/male/James M. Willson/Susan
Willson/farmer/1866 Jan 30

1865 Nov 10/Smithville/Edwin S. Wright/male/Richard H. Wright/Mary E. Wright/
farmer/1866 Feb 10

1866 Feb 20/near Preston/James W. Wright/male/Jesse Wright/Ann Emily Wright/
farmer/1866 Apr 10

Birth

1865 Nov 17/near Denton/___/male/John L. Willis/Annie Willis/farmer/1866 Apr 23

1865 Dec 11/near Denton/___/male/William H. Wooters/Martha E. Wooters/farmer/
1866 Apr 23

1865 Nov 30/Boonsborough/Frank Edwin Williams/male/Thomas S. Williams/Mary
Emily Williams/farmer/1866 Apr 28

1866 Mar 24/near Preston/Herby Wright/male/Curtis Wright/Lydia P. Wright/
farmer/1866 May 8

1865 Aug 6/near Federalsburg/Willard Williamson/William H. Williamson/Mary
Jane Williamson/farmer/1866 May 12

1866 Jan 1/near Federalsburg/John Henry Williamson/male/Cartis A. Williamson/
Sarah Ann Williamson/farmer/1866 May 12

1865 Dec 23/Preston/Henry Noble Willis/male/Henry F. Willis/Emily R. Willis/
physician 1866 May 23

1866 Feb 25/Fowling Creek/William P. Willis/male/Peter Willis Jr/Martha
Willis/farmer/1866 Aug 3

1866 Mar 10/near Preston/John Edward Wright/male/John R. Wright/Ann Wright/
farmer/1866 Aug 14

1865 Jul 27/near Preston/Celestial Ann Cooper Webb/female/Black/John E. Webb/
Mary C. Webb/farmer/1866 Sep 12

1866 May 9/near Bloomery/Eugene C. Wright/male/Lewis B. Wright/Sarah Wright/
farmer/1866 Nov 13

1867 Mar 3/near Preston/William Elwood Waddell/male/William B. Waddell/
Elizabeth E. Waddell/farmer/1867 Apr 6

1866 Dec 7/near New Hope P. O./Harvey Willis/male/Francis A. Willis/Sallie E.
Willis/school teacher/1867 Apr 23

1865 Feb 3/near New Hope P.O./Clara Willis/female/Francis A. Willis/Sallie E.
Willis/school teacher/1867 Apr 23

1867 Jun 21/near Preston/Mary Hester Webb/female/Black/John E. Webb/Mary C.
Webb/farmer/1867 Jul 29

1866 Apr 29/near Denton/Mary Lucretia Willoughby/female/Aaron Willoughby/Mary
Willoughby/farmer/1867 Dec 16

1867 Mar 21/near Denton/___Willson/female/Lewis Willson/Sallie Willson/miller/
1867 Dec 16

1867 Jan 16/near Bridgetown/Kate V. Willoughby/female/George M. Willoughby/
Sarah M. Willoughby/none/1867 Dec 17

1867 Feb 14/___/Peter B. Wright/male/Peter Wright of William/Priscilla Wright/
-/1867 Dec 21

1866 May 9/Smithville/Eugene C. Wright/male/Lewis B. Wright/Sarah A. Wright/
mechanic/1867 Dec 24

1867 Nov 6/near Friendship/John W. Williams/male/William Williams/Sarah E.
Williams/farmer/1868 Jan 7

1866 Nov 10/Tuckahoe Neck/Emma B. Williams/female/William A. Williams/
Caroline Williams/farmer/1868 Feb 11

State Records of Death and Birth

<u>Birth</u>

1866 Nov 26/Tuckahoe Neck/Ida Williams/female/Robert D. Williams/Ann Maria Williams/farmer/1868 Feb 11

1867 Aug 21/Tuckahoe Neck/Anna Davis Wilson/female/Robert H. Wilson/Carrie K. Wilson/merchant/1868 Feb 18

1867 Oct 5/near Preston/Daniel E. Wright/male/Daniel R. Wright/Mary E. Wright/farmer/1868 Apr 21

1868 Mar 31/near Bloomery/Charles Elmer Wright/male/Richard H. Wright/Mary E. Wright/farmer/1869 Feb 9

1869 Feb 6/Tuckahoe Neck/___/female/William A. Williams/-/farmer/1869 Mar 4

1868 Jan 19/near Smithville/___/male/Lewis B. Wright/Sarah Wright/wheelwright/1869 Sep 21

1869 Feb 1/near Smithville/Mary E. Wright/female/Lewis Wright/Sarah Wright/wheelwright/1869 Sep 21

1869 Mar 12/near Union Corner/Lilly May Wright/female/Trustin M. Wright/Julia Wright/farmer/1869 Dec 8

1869 Nov 14/-/John Milton Willis/male/Peter Willis/Martha Willis/1870 Apr 8

1869 Nov 23/near Preston/Eliza Ann Wright/female/Daniel R. Wright/Mary E. Wright/farmer/1870 Sep 23

1870 Jun 7/near Smithville/Levin B. Wright/male/Lewis B. Wright/Sarah Wright/wheelwright/1870 Dec 20

1866 Mar 19/near Denton/___/female/Jacob L. Zook/Levina Zook/farmer/1866 Apr 23

INDEX ·

DECOURSEY Hestor 74
DEEN Lacy 71
DEFORD Amanda 32, W. 32
DENNY Stephen 26
DEROCHBRUNE Thomas 31
DERONDE Jennie E. 56
DESHIELDS Florence 60
DEVINNEY M. Onie 25
DEWEESE Draper A. 27,
William H. 27, 60
DEWING T. S. 63,
William 63
DICK A. D. 45, 47(2),
48, 49, 53, 55, John R.
87, Mary 87
DICKERSON Joshua 76
DILL ___ 75, Emma S.
31, Eugene 26, Hester
A. 56, J. R. 40, 48,
55, 61, James R. 31,
John T. 69, Mary 12,
Mary S. 61
DILLEN John A. 38,
Sarah 38
DILLIN John A. 49
DISHAROON Ella C. 8
DIXON Annie E. 55,
Elenor 29, James A. 55,
Mamie C. 46
DOBBS Lillian A. 73
DONE Babeck S. 72
DONNELLY J. O. 77
DOOD John N. 12
DORSEY F. G. 30
DOUGLAS Amanda 93,
James E. 65, James K.
93, Mary C. 65, 76,
Mary E. 93
DOUGLASS Harry Field
46, J. H. 36, James E.
7, James H. 56, Joseph
35, Mary Catharine 56,
Mary E. 56
DOWLING Edward 62
DOWN Edward L. 24
DOWNES A. H. 80, Anna
H. 15, 87, Annie Estell
42, Annie H. 42, 87(2),
Annie L. 22, Annie M.
10, Benjamin A. 69,
Bennett 31, Dr. 74,
Edith 78, Edward
Hardcastle 80, 87, Ida
54, J. W. 87, James S.

29, John W. 29, Josephine
57, Lola W. 87, Louisianna
87, P. W. 42, 54, 80,
Philip Alvon 15, Philip W.
10, 15, 87, 87, Raymond
10, Raymond Worthington
87, Reynor B. 47, Sallie
63, Stephen R. 44, William
H. 54, 74, William T. 17,
87
DOWNHAM John 40
DOWNS Clair 69, John W.
72, Susanna 36, William 73
DRAPER Emma 35, Laura 80,
Laura Grant 20, Margaret
A. 18, 70, Margaret Ann
20, Peter 18, 20, Sarah
80, T. H. 80
DRIFFIS William 45
DRIVER Joseph 75
DUDLEY C. 74
DUESSE William H. 39
DUFFY Anna E. 87,
Catharine 87(4), Hugh
87(3), Hugh Clarence 87
DUHADAWAY W. J. 24, 28,
32(2), 35, 36, J. W. 37
DUHADWAY H. L. 32, Ruliff
L. 32
DUKES Agnes Josephine 22,
Boon 14, Caroline 75,
Charles G. 87, Charles
Griffith 87, Clara Bell
87, Ellen 33, James 25,
James B. 14, J. Boon 22,
87, Jesse 54, John B. 87,
John H. 4, 80, Josephine
32, Levi 1, 27(2), Low 22,
Maria L. 87, Margaret A. 5,
Melissa 87, Miss ___ 56,
Sarah 77, Sarah B. 51,
Sarah E. 87, Susan 27,
Thomas 56
DULING Thomas H. 34
DUNHAM Sarah A. 43
DUNNELLY F. Olin 72
DUNNING Bessie 28, Charles
A. 18, 20, 28, 65, 87,
Charles Percival 87, E. T.
61, Ella 28, 65, Ella M.
87, Laurence 65, Mary B.
20(2), Rebecca A. 21,
Samuel 20, 80, Taner(?) 80
DYER Henrietta 40, William

40, William H. 40

EARICKSON Sara 24,
Thomas J. 24, 50
EATON ___ 10, 68,
Elisha 38, Ezekiel 88,
George 88, H. F. 40,
Jacob Spencer 88, John
F. 3, Levice Ann 88,
Litha Jane 88,
Marietta 88, Mary 46,
Nancy Bell 88, Robert
13, T. C. 56, Thomas
3, 56, Thomas J. 51,
W. E. 55, William 88,
Wilmina 88
ECKNER Mary A. 54
EDGAR Thomas 43
EDGELL Emily 20
EDWARDS James S. 7,
Rev 55
ELDERDICE J. M. 64
ELDERICE J. M. 62
ELIOTT Rev 16
ELLIOTT C. H. 45,
Elias T. 34, Laura A.
77, W. 49, William T.
5
ELLWANGER Hartley 70
EMERSON Elizabeth R.
70, J. H. 21, J.
Marion 4, 15, 19, 24,
John Clarence 88,
John H. 18, 88(2),
J. Marion 88, Lizza
19, Lizzie Roberta 15,
88, Lizzie S. 15, 24,
88(2), Maria 80, 88,
Maria L. 8, Marion
Clinton 19, 70, Mary
Luretta 88, R. R. 11,
31, Rebecca A. 88(2),
Robert 1(2), Robert R.
8, 88, Samuel 55,
Sarah 70, Sarah E. 55,
Sarah L. 18, Walter 31
EMMERICH C. W. 55,
Charles W. 54
EMORY John 66
ENGLAND E. 3, Rev 65,
W. E. 2
ERVIN John 45
ERWIN J. 39, John 11,
24

-101-

INDEX

HAYDEN Daniel 17
HAYMAN William T. 35
HAYWARD Colonel 61,
Willie 61
HEATHER Gulia 31, Julia
31, Thomas E. 31(2),
Thomas Emory 31, Thomas
Leonard 31
HENCHY Rev 37, 43, 44,
49
HENDRICKSON Jacob 50
HENRY Frank 58, 72
HEPBRON S. S. 54
HERITAGE George 8
HEWITT Rev 16
HICKS James 38, 68,
John 67, Robert 69
HIGGINS Sussie 13
HIGNUTT Charles H. 55,
Charles W. 46, J. W.
41, James 58, 63, James
W. 39, Martha J. 39, N.
Elizabeth 41, Peter W.
39
HILL Charles 40, 43,
49, Joseph 56
HINES A. W. 10, William
78
HINSON Elizabeth 46
HITCH Arena 54, Arthur
56, Esrah 1, Samuel S.
14
HOBB George T. 35,
Benjamin 73, Francis J.
3, Howard S. 46,
Margaret Ellen 13
HOCKING Dr. 73
HODGES Martha 69
HOFF William Walter 18
HOFFECKER E. H. 43
HOLBROOK Emma E. 35,
William A. 35
HOLLIDAY Edward 51,
Thomas 15
HOLLINGSWORTH William
34
HOLLIS George H. 16,
William H. 22
HOLLYDAY Mary 47
HOLMES Rev 31, 32, W.
G. 22(2), William 10
HOLT Bessie Virginia
45, 46, Grace A. 45,
James W. 45, K. E. 32,

Mary Seth 32, T. S. 32,
Thomas 78
HOPKINS Annie 62, Emma
65, Fannie 13, J. 62,
Lida B. 44, Matilda 58,
Nicholas S. 7, Samuel 62,
Samuel R. 30, Samuel T.
13, Susie 11
HOPPER Ann 2, Lou D. 59,
P. B. 2
HORBOGEN Quintus 58
HORNER H. C. 47
HORNEY J. E. 50, 54, 56
HORSEY Clara 89,
Elizabeth 4, Ellen 33,
Ellen M. 23, Eva 50,
Henry 54, Jacob 13, James
H. 12, John 89, John H.
13, 19, Lida 22, Margaret
13, Maria Louise 89, Mary
Ellen 54, Nathaniel 29,
Revel 10, Ruth 89,
Samuel H. 23, 33, Turpin
73, Turpin Moore 54,
William 13, William G.
50, 89
HOUGH J. 6(2), 7, 8, John
3(3), 4(2), 50, Walter 70
HOWARD Frederick 30
HOXTER Anna E. 1
HUBBARD Armilla 26,
Catharine 81, Chaney 12,
Christiana 26, Christina
25, Elizabeth 46, Ennalls
21, 53, 74, Eugene 23,
Francis M. 54, Frank 18,
James 56, 69, James H.
81(2), 89, James Henry
89, James J. 80, James P.
T. 89, Jesse 6, 39, 40,
51, 76, 84, Jesse H. T.
9, Josephine 56, Lemuel
81, Martha 7, 89, Mary
18, 21, 71, Michael 81,
Millie 25, Mrs. 3, Nancy
80, Nancy C. 89, Ortera
48, Poulson 26, Poulson
E. 65, Thomas 18, 81, W.
E. 47, Wenna Blades 89,
William 3, William J. 18
HUDSON Samuel H. 35,
William H. 68
HUGHES Elizabeth 62,
Samuel 62

HULL Annie A. 53
HUMPHREY Daniel 81,
Mary 81, Mary E. 81
HUMPHREYS Eugene W. 16
HUNGERFORD Florence V.
30
HUNTER W. 48
HUNTINGTON C. 64
HURLOCK Annie B. 33,
Sarah A. 41
HUTCHINS J. T. 36,
Nicey 77, Ormand 36,
W. H. 34
HUTCHINSON A. L. 89,
Andrew L. 4, Azeb T.
56, Caroline 32, Lydia
42, Manlius 42, Mary
Virginia 89, Wilmina
89, Winona 35
HUTSON Catharine 40
HYNSON Charles 43,
Clarsy 74, E. H. 22,
30, 31, 35, 36, 38,
41, 44, 45, Harry W.
58, Henry W. 59, J. T.
51, 58, James T. 3,
M. M. 37, Martha C.
58, William 43,
William R. 19

ING Melinda 19
INSLEY Sallie 35
IRVIN Henry 90
IRWIN John 3

JACKSON Ella 47, Rev
19, Sarah F. 42
JAMES Ann 67, Anna 71,
E. H. S. 59, Fleming
30, Joseph F. 32,
Millie A. 32, William
D. 56
JARMAN Emma 35.
JARREL Robert 65
JARRELL C. E. 66,
Henry 32, James 3,
John 37, Laurel V. 50,
Lavinia 14, Maggie 11,
Margaret 32, Robert
43, Thomas 14, 21
JEFFERSON Dr. 76
JENKINS Dr. 43, George
Bascom 90, Rebecca 90,
Walter F. 75

-104-

INDEX

INDEX

INDEX

Heritage Books by F. Edward Wright:

Abstracts of Bucks County, Pennsylvania Wills, 1685–1785

Abstracts of Cumberland County, Pennsylvania Wills, 1750–1785

Abstracts of Cumberland County, Pennsylvania Wills, 1785–1825

Abstracts of Philadelphia County Wills, 1726–1747

Abstracts of Philadelphia County Wills, 1748–1763

Abstracts of Philadelphia County Wills, 1763–1784

Abstracts of Philadelphia County Wills, 1777–1790

Abstracts of Philadelphia County Wills, 1790–1802

Abstracts of Philadelphia County Wills, 1802–1809

Abstracts of Philadelphia County Wills, 1810–1815

Abstracts of Philadelphia County Wills, 1815–1819

Abstracts of Philadelphia County Wills, 1820–1825

Abstracts of Philadelphia County, Pennsylvania Wills, 1682–1726

Abstracts of South Central Pennsylvania Newspapers, Volume 1, 1785–1790

Abstracts of South Central Pennsylvania Newspapers, Volume 3, 1796–1800

Abstracts of the Newspapers of Georgetown and the Federal City, 1789–99

Abstracts of York County, Pennsylvania Wills, 1749–1819

*Bucks County, Pennsylvania Church Records of the 17th and 18th Centuries
Volume 2: Quaker Records: Falls and Middletown Monthly Meetings*
Anna Miller Watring and F. Edward Wright

Caroline County, Maryland Marriages, Births and Deaths, 1850–1880

Citizens of the Eastern Shore of Maryland, 1659–1750

Cumberland County, Pennsylvania Church Records of the 18th Century

Delaware Newspaper Abstracts, Volume 1: 1786–1795

Early Charles County, Maryland Settlers, 1658–1745
Marlene Strawser Bates and F. Edward Wright

Early Church Records of Alexandria City and Fairfax County, Virginia
F. Edward Wright and Wesley E. Pippenger

Early Church Records of New Castle County, Delaware, Volume 1, 1701–1800

Frederick County Militia in the War of 1812
Sallie A. Mallick and F. Edward Wright

Inhabitants of Baltimore County, 1692–1763

Land Records of Sussex County, Delaware, 1769–1782

Land Records of Sussex County, Delaware, 1782–1789
Elaine Hastings Mason and F. Edward Wright

Marriage Licenses of Washington, District of Columbia, 1811–1830

*Marriages and Deaths from the Newspapers of Allegany and
Washington Counties, Maryland, 1820–1830*

Marriages and Deaths from The York Recorder, 1821–1830

*Marriages and Deaths in the Newspapers of Frederick and
Montgomery Counties, Maryland, 1820–1830*